DATA LITERACY
WITH
PYTHON

DATA LITERACY
WITH
PYTHON

Oswald Campesato

MERCURY LEARNING AND INFORMATION
Boston, Massachusetts

Publisher: David Pallai
MERCURY LEARNING AND INFORMATION
121 High Street, 3rd Floor
Boston, MA 02110
info@merclearning.com
www.merclearning.com
800-232-0223

O. Campesato. *Data Literacy with Python.*
ISBN 978-1-50152-199-7

The publisher recognizes and respects all marks used by companies, manufacturers, and developers as a means to distinguish their products. All brand names and product names mentioned in this book are trademarks or service marks of their respective companies. Any omission or misuse (of any kind) of service marks or trademarks, etc. is not an attempt to infringe on the property of others.

Library of Congress Control Number: 2023945518

232425321   This book is printed on acid-free paper in the United States of America.

Our titles are available for adoption, license, or bulk purchase by institutions, corporations, etc. For additional information, please contact the Customer Service Dept. at 800-232-0223(toll free).

All of our titles are available in digital format at academiccourseware.com and other digital vendors. *Companion files (code listings) for this title are available by contacting info@merclearning.com.* The sole obligation of MERCURY LEARNING AND INFORMATION to the purchaser is to replace the disc, based on defective materials or faulty workmanship, but not based on the operation or functionality of the product.

I'd like to dedicate this book to my parents
– may this bring joy and happiness into their lives.

CONTENTS

PREFACE

The purpose of this book is to usher readers into the world of data, ensuring a comprehensive understanding of its nuances, intricacies, and complexities. With Python 3 as the primary medium, the book underscores the pivotal role of data in modern industries, and how its adept management can lead to insightful decision-making.

THE CORE PROPOSITION

At its heart, the book provides a swift introduction to foundational data-related tasks, priming the readers for more advanced concepts of model training introduced later on. Through detailed, step-by-step Python code examples, the readers will traverse the journey of training models, beginning with the kNN algorithm, and then smoothly transitioning to other classifiers, effortlessly, by tweaking mere lines of code.

FROM BASICS TO VISUALIZATION

The narrative commences with a dive into datasets and potential issues, gradually segueing into more intricate topics like anomaly detection and data cleaning. As one progresses, the guide unfolds the intricacies of classification algorithms, followed by a deep dive into data visualization. Here, tools like Sweetviz, Skimpy, Matplotlib, and Seaborn are introduced, offering readers a hands-on experience in rendering charts and graphs.

TECHNICAL PREREQUISITES

To derive the maximum value from this book, a foundational grasp of Python 3.x is requisite. While some sections might necessitate a preliminary understanding of the 'awk' utility, the majority of the content is dedicated to Python's prowess. Familiarity with Pandas, especially its data frames, will further enhance the reader's journey.

CODE VARIETIES

Appreciating the diversity in learning styles, the book encapsulates a blend of short, detailed, and progressive code samples. This variety ensures that whether one is a hands-on coder, who jumps straight into execution, or a contemplative reader, who ponders over logic, there's something for everyone.

GLOBAL AUDIENCE, GLOBAL LANGUAGE

Designed for individuals beginning their foray into machine learning, the language caters to a global audience. By intentionally steering clear of colloquialisms, and adopting a standard English approach, it ensures content clarity for readers, irrespective of their linguistic backgrounds.

THE ESSENCE OF THE CODE

While the enclosed code samples are comprehensive, their essence lies in their clarity. They are meticulously designed to elucidate the underlying concepts rather than emphasize efficiency or brevity. However, readers are encouraged to optimize, experiment, and improvise, making the code their own.

Companion files with source code and data sets are available by writing to the publisher at info@merclearning.com.

BEYOND THE CODE

While "Data Literacy with Python" is predominantly a technical guide, it champions the idea that the most potent tool is a curious mind. A genuine intrigue for data, complemented by the determination to decipher code samples, is what will make this journey truly transformative.

O. Campesato
October 2023

WORKING WITH DATA

This chapter shows you how to analyze data types that you will encounter in datasets, such as currency and dates, as well as scaling data values in order to ensure that a dataset has "clean" data.

The first part of this chapter briefly discusses some aspects of EDA (exploratory data analysis), such as data quality, data-centric AI versus model-centric AI, as well as some of the steps involved in data cleaning and data wrangling. You will also see an EDA code sample involving the Titanic dataset.

The second part of this chapter describes common types of data, such as binary, nominal, ordinal, and categorical data. In addition, you will learn about continuous versus discrete data, quantitative and quantitative data, and types of statistical data.

The third second introduces the notion of data drift and data leakage, followed by model selection. This section also describes how to process categorical data, and how to map categorical data to numeric data.

Keep in mind that the code samples in this chapter utilize NumPy and Pandas, both of which are discussed in a corresponding appendix.

WHAT IS DATA LITERACY?

There are various definitions of data literacy that involve concepts such as data, meaningful information, decision-making, drawing conclusions, chart reading, and so forth. According to Wikipedia, which we'll use as a starting point, *data literacy* is defined as follows:

> Data literacy is the ability to read, understand, create, and communicate data as information. Much like literacy as a general concept, data literacy focuses on the competencies involved in

working with data. It is, however, not similar to the ability to read text since it requires certain skills involving reading and understanding data. (Wikipedia, 2023)

Data literacy encompasses many topics, starting with analyzing data that is often in the form of a CSV (comma-separated values) file. The quality of the data in a dataset is of paramount importance: high data quality enables you to make more reliable inferences regarding the nature of the data. Indeed, high data quality is a requirement for fields such as machine learning, scientific experiments, and so forth. However, keep in mind that you might face various challenges regarding robust data, such as:

- a limited amount of available data
- costly acquisition of relevant data
- difficulty in generating valid synthetic data
- availability of domain experts

Depending on the domain, the cost of data cleaning can involve months of work at a cost of millions of dollars. For instance, identifying images of cats and dogs is essentially trivial, whereas identifying potential tumors in x-rays is much more costly and requires highly skilled individuals.

With all the preceding points in mind, let's take a look at EDA (exploratory data analysis), which is the topic of the next section.

EXPLORATORY DATA ANALYSIS (EDA)

According to Wikipedia, EDA involves analyzing datasets to summarize their main characteristics, often with visual methods. EDA also involves searching through data to detect patterns (if there are any) and anomalies, and in some cases, test hypotheses regarding the distribution of the data.

EDA represents the initial phase of data analysis, whereby data is explored in order to determine its primary characteristics. Moreover, this phase involves detecting patterns (if any), and any outstanding issues pertaining to the data. The purpose of EDA is to obtain an understanding of the semantics of the data without performing a deep assessment of the nature of the data. The analysis is often performed through data visualization in order to produce a summary of their most important characteristics. The four types of EDA are listed here:

- univariate nongraphical
- multivariate nongraphical
- univariate graphical
- multivariate graphical

In brief, the two primary methods for data analysis are *qualitative data analysis* techniques and *quantitative data analysis* techniques.

As an example of exploratory data analysis, consider the plethora of cell phones that customers can purchase for various needs (work, home, minors, and so forth). Visualize the data in an associated dataset to determine the top ten (or top three) most popular cell phones, which can potentially be performed by state (or province) and country.

An example of quantitative data analysis involves measuring (quantifying) data, which can be gathered from physical devices, surveys, or activities such as downloading applications from a Web page.

Common visualization techniques used in EDA include histograms, line graphs, bar charts, box plots, and multivariate charts.

What Is Data Quality?

According to Wikipedia, *data quality* refers to "the state of qualitative or quantitative pieces of information" (Wikipedia, 2022). Furthermore, high data quality refers to data whose quality meets the various needs of an organization. In particular, performing data cleaning tasks are the type of tasks that assist in achieving high data quality.

When companies label their data, they obviously strive for a high quality of labeled data, and yet the quality can be adversely affected in various ways, some of which are as follows:

- inaccurate methodology for labeling data
- insufficient data accuracy
- insufficient attention to data management

The cumulative effect of the preceding (and other) types of errors can be significant, to the extent that models underperform in a production environment. In addition to the technical aspects, underperforming models can have an adverse effect on business revenue.

Related to data quality is *data quality assurance*, which typically involves data cleaning tasks that are discussed later in this chapter, after which data is analyzed to detect potential inconsistencies in the data, and then determine how to resolve those inconsistencies. Another aspect to consider: the aggregation of additional data sources, especially involving heterogenous sources of data, can introduce challenges with respect to ensuring data quality. Other concepts related to data quality include *data stewardship* and *data governance*, both of which are discussed in multiple online articles.

Data-Centric AI or Model-Centric AI?

A *model-centric* approach focuses primarily on enhancing the performance of a given model, and data considered secondary in importance. In fact, during the past ten years or so, the emphasis of AI has been a model-centric approach. Note that during this time span some very powerful models and architectures have been developed, such as the CNN model for image classification in 2012 and the enormous impact (especially in NLP) of models based on the transformer architecture that was developed in 2017.

By contrast, a *data-centric* approach concentrates on improving data, which relies on several factors, such as the quality of labels for the data as well as obtaining accurate data for training a model.

Given the importance of high-quality data with respect to training a model, it stands to reason that using a data-centric approach instead of a model-centric approach can result in higher quality models in AI. While data quality and model effectiveness are both important, keep in mind that the data-centric approach is becoming increasingly more strategic in the machine learning world. More information can be found on the AI Multiple site: *https://research.aimultiple.com/data-centric-ai/*

The Data Cleaning and Data Wrangling Steps

The next step often involves *data cleaning* in order to find and correct errors in the dataset, such as missing data, duplicate data, or invalid data. This task also involves data consistency, which pertains to updating different representations of the same value in a consistent manner. As a simple example, suppose that a Web page contains a form with an input field whose valid input is either Y or N, but users are able to enter Yes, Ys, or ys as text input. Obviously, these values correspond to the value Y, and they must all be converted to the same value in order to achieve data consistency.

Finally, *data wrangling* can be performed after the data cleaning task is completed. Although interpretations of data wrangling do vary, in this book the term refers to transforming datasets into different formats as well as combining two or more datasets. Hence, data wrangling does not examine the individual data values to determine whether or not they are valid: this step is performed during data cleaning.

Keep in mind that sometimes it's worthwhile to perform another data cleaning step after the data wrangling step. For example, suppose that two CSV files contain employee-related data, and you merge these CSV files into a third CSV file. The newly created CSV file might contain duplicate values: it's certainly possible to have two people with the same name (such as John Smith), which obviously needs to be resolved.

ELT and ETL

ELT is an acronym for extract, load, and transform, which is a pipeline-based approach for managing data. Another pipeline-based approach is called ETL (extract, transform, load), which is actually more popular than ELT. However, ELT has the following advantages over ETL:

- ELT requires less computational time.
- ELT is well-suited for processing large datasets.
- ELT is more cost effective than ETL.

ELT involves (1) data extraction from one or more sources, (2) transforming the raw data into a suitable format, and (3) loading the result into a data warehouse. The data in the warehouse becomes available for additional analysis.

WHERE DO WE FIND DATA?

Data resides in many locations, with different formats, languages, and currencies. An important task involves finding the sources of relevant data and then aggregating that data in a meaningful fashion. Some examples of sources of data are as follows:

- CSV/TSV files
- RBDMS tables
- NoSQL tables
- Web Services

The following subsections briefly describe some of the details that are involved with each of the items in the preceding bullet list.

Working With CSV Files

A CSV file (comma-separated values) or TSV file (tab-separated values) is a common source of data, and other delimiters (semi-colons, "#" symbols, and so forth) can also appear in a text file with data. Moreover, you might need to combine multiple CSV files into a single file that contains the data to perform an accurate analysis.

As a simple example, the following snippet displays a portion of the `titanic.csv` dataset:

```
survived,pclass,sex,age,sibsp,parch,fare,embarked,
class,who,adult_male,deck,embark_town,alive,alone
0,3,male,22.0,1,0,7.25,S,Third,man,True,,Southampton,
no,False
1,1,female,38.0,1,0,71.2833,C,First,woman,False,C,
Cherbourg,yes,False
1,3,female,26.0,0,0,7.925,S,Third,woman,False,,
Southampton,yes,True
```

As you can see, there are many columns (also called "features") in the preceding set of data. When you perform machine learning, you need to determine which of those columns provide meaningful data. Notice the survived attribute: this is known as the *target feature*, which contains the values that you are trying to predict correctly. The prediction of who survives is based on identifying the columns (features) that are relevant in making such a prediction.

For example, the sex, age, and class features are most likely relevant for determining whether or not a passenger survived the fate of the Titanic. How do you know if you have selected all the relevant features, and only the relevant features?

There are two main techniques for doing so. In some datasets it's possible to visually inspect the features of a dataset in order to determine the most important features. Loosely speaking, when you "eyeball" the data to determine the set of relevant features, that's called *feature selection*. This approach can be viable when there is a relatively small number of features in the dataset (i.e., ten or fewer features).

On the other hand, it's very difficult to visually determine the relevant features in a dataset that contains 5,000 columns. Fortunately, you can use an algorithm such as PCA (Principal Component Analysis) to determine which features are significant. The use of such an algorithm (and there are others as well) is called *feature extraction*.

Moreover, it's important to enlist the aid of a so-called domain expert (which might be you) who can assist in determining the most important features of a dataset, and also determine if there are any missing features that are important in the selection of features.

Working With RDBMS Data

An RDBMS (relational database management system) stores data in a structured manner by utilizing database tables whose structure is defined by you. For example, suppose that you have an online store that sells products, and you want to keep track of customers, purchase orders, and inventory.

One approach involves defining a customer's table, which has the following (simplified) type of structure:

```
CREATE TABLE customers (
cust_id INTEGER,
first_name VARCHAR(20),
last_name VARCHAR(20),
home_address VARCHAR(20),
city VARCHAR(20),
state VARCHAR(20),
zip_code VARCHAR(10));
```

Next, you can use SQL (structured query language) statements in order to insert data into the customers table, as shown here:

```
INSERT INTO customers
VALUES (1000,'John','Smith','123 Main St',
'Fremont','CA','94123');


INSERT INTO customers
VALUES (2000,'Jane','Jones','456 Front St',
'Fremont','CA','95015');
```

In a real application you obviously need real data, which you can gather from a Web registration page that enables users to register for your Web application (we'll skip those details).

If you use an RDBMS such as MySQL, you can define a database and database tables, such as the customers table described previously. The following SQL statement displays the structure of the customers table that was defined previously:

```
mysql> DESCRIBE customers;
+---------+----------+------+-----+---------+-------+
| Field   | Type     | Null | Key | Default | Extra |
+---------+----------+------+-----+---------+-------+
| cust_id | int      | YES  |     | NULL    |       |
| name    | char(30) | YES  |     | NULL    |       |
| address | char(30) | YES  |     | NULL    |       |
| email   | char(30) | YES  |     | NULL    |       |
+---------+----------+------+-----+---------+-------+
4 rows in set (0.03 sec)
```

After manually inserting data with a SQL INSERT statement, you can also select the data from the customers table via a SQL SELECT statement, as shown here (the simulated data is different from the previous data):

```
mysql> SELECT * FROM customers;
+---------+----------------+-------------------------
---+---------------------------+
| cust_id | name           | address
| email                     |
+---------+----------------+-------------------------
---+---------------------------+
|     100 | Jaime Peterson | 17228 Kelli Cliffs Apt.
625 | clinejohnathan@hotmail.com |
|     200 | Mark Smith     | 729 Cassandra Isle Apt.
768 | brandon36@hotmail.com      |
|     300 | Patrick Pacheco | 84460 Griffith Loaf
| charles61@proctor.com      |
|     400 | Justin Owens   | 2221 Renee Villages
| kyates@myers.com           |
+---------+----------------+-------------------------
---+---------------------------+
4 rows in set (0.00 sec)
```

In simplified terms, an RDBMS involves the following tasks:

- Define the relevant tables
- Insert meaningful data into the tables
- Select useful data from the tables

One way to insert data involves programmatically loading data from CSV files into the database tables. An RDBMS provides many useful features, which includes exporting the data from all the tables in a database, and the export file can be a single SQL file that contains all the SQL statements that are required for creating the relevant tables and inserting existing data (i.e., data that you already inserted) into those tables.

You also need a purchase orders table to keep track of which customers have made purchases from your store. An example of the structure of a purchase orders table is shown here:

```
mysql> DESCRIBE purch_orders;
+-----------+------+------+-----+---------+-------+
| Field     | Type | Null | Key | Default | Extra |
+-----------+------+------+-----+---------+-------+
| cust_id   | int  | YES  |     | NULL    |       |
| purch_id  | int  | YES  |     | NULL    |       |
| line_item | int  | YES  |     | NULL    |       |
+-----------+------+------+-----+---------+-------+
3 rows in set (0.01 sec)
```

Notice that each row in the purch_orders table contains a cust_id and a purch_id column: that's because a purchase order is associated with a customer, and a customer can place one or more purchase orders. In database parlance, the customers table has a one-to-many relationship with the purchase orders table, and every row in the latter table must have an associated row in the customers table (and those that do not are called "orphans").

In fact, there is also a one-to-many relationship between the purchase orders table and the item_desc table, where the latter contains information about each product that was purchased in a given purchase order. Note that each row in a purchase order is called a *line item*.

Working With NoSQL Data

A NoSQL database is useful when the data that you manage does not have a fixed structure. Examples of popular NoSQL databases are MongoDB and Cassandra.

Instead of defining a fixed structure for tables, you can populate a NoSQL database dynamically with documents, where documents belong to a *collection* instead of a table. Obviously, documents can have different lengths and contain different text, which can be conveniently stored and accessed in a collection in a NoSQL database.

DEALING WITH DATA: WHAT CAN GO WRONG?

In a perfect world, all datasets are in pristine condition, with no extreme values, no missing values, and no erroneous values. Every feature value is captured correctly, with no chance for any confusion. Moreover, no conversion is required between date formats, currency values, or languages because of the one universal standard that defines the correct formats and acceptable values for every possible set of data values.

However, you cannot rely on the scenarios in the previous paragraph, which is the reason for the techniques that are discussed in this chapter. Even after you manage to create a wonderfully clean and robust dataset, other issues can arise, such as data drift that is described in the next section.

In fact, the task of cleaning data is not necessarily complete even after a machine learning model is deployed to a production environment. For instance, an online system that gathers terabytes or petabytes of data on a daily basis can contain skewed values that in turn adversely affect the performance of the model. Such adverse effects can be revealed through the changes in the metrics that are associated with the production model.

Datasets

In simple terms, a *dataset* is a source of data (such as a text file) that contains rows and columns of data. Each row is typically called a "data point," and each column is called a "feature". A dataset can be a CSV (comma separated values), TSV (tab separated values), Excel spreadsheet, a table in an RDMBS, a document in a NoSQL database, the output from a Web service, and so forth.

Note that a *static dataset* consists of fixed data. For example, a CSV file that contains the states of the United States is a static dataset. A slightly different example involves a product table that contains information about the products that customers can buy from a company. Such a table is static if no new products are added to the table. Discontinued products are probably maintained as historical data that can appear in product-related reports.

By contrast, a *dynamic dataset* consists of data that changes over a period of time. Simple examples include housing prices, stock prices, and time-based data from IoT devices.

A dataset can vary from very small (perhaps a few features and 100 rows) to very large (more than 1,000 features and more than one million rows). If you are unfamiliar with the problem domain for a particular dataset, then you might struggle to determine its most important features. In this situation, you consult a "domain expert" who understands the importance of the features, their interdependencies (if any), and whether or not the data values for the features are valid. In addition, there are algorithms (called dimensionality reduction algorithms) that can help you determine the most important features, such as PCA (Principal Component Analysis).

Before delving into topics such as data preprocessing, data types, and so forth, let's take a brief detour to introduce the concept of feature importance, which is the topic of the next section.

As you will see, someone needs to analyze the dataset to determine which features are the most important and which features can be safely ignored in order to train a model with the given dataset. A dataset can contain various data types, such as:

- audio data
- image data
- numeric data
- text-based data
- video data
- combinations of the above

In this book, we'll only consider datasets that contain columns with numeric or text-based data types, which can be further classified as follows:

- nominal (string-based or numeric)
- ordinal (ordered values)
- categorical (enumeration)
- interval (positive/negative values)
- ratio (nonnegative values)

The next section contains brief descriptions of the data types that are in the preceding bullet list.

EXPLANATION OF DATA TYPES

This section contains subsections that provide brief descriptions about the following data types:

- binary data
- nominal data
- ordinal data
- categorical data
- interval data
- ratio data

Later you will learn about the difference between continuous data versus discrete data, as well as the difference between qualitative data versus quantitative data. In addition, the `Pandas` documentation describes data types and how to use them in `Python`.

Binary Data

Binary data involves data that can only take two distinct values. As such, binary data is the simplest type of data. A common example involves flipping a fair coin: the only outcomes are in the set `{H,T}`. Other terms for binary data include dichotomous, logical data, Boolean data, and indicator data. Binary data is also a type of categorical data that is discussed later.

Nominal Data

The word "nominal" has multiple meanings, and in our case, it refers to something that constitutes a name (the prefix "nom" means "name"). Thus, *nominal data* is often (see next paragraph) name-based data that involves different name labels. Examples of nominal data include: hair color, music preferences, movie types, and so forth. As you can see, there is no hierarchy or ordering involved, so all values have the same importance. However, the number of items in nominal values might be different, such as the number of people that belong to different political parties.

Nominal data can involve numeric values to represent different values of a feature. For example, the numbers in the set `{0,1}` can represent `{Male, Female}`, and the numbers in the set `{0,1,2,3,4,5,6}` can represent the days in a week. However, there is no hierarchical interpretation associated with these numeric values: the day of the week represented by "0" is not considered more important or more valuable than any of the other numeric labels for the other days of the week. Instead, think of each element in terms of its predecessor and successor: note that the first element has no predecessor, and the last element has no successor. If you are familiar with programming languages, the counterpart to integer-based nominal values would be an enumeration, an example of which is here:

```
enum DAY {SUN,MON,TUE,WED,THU,FRI,SAT};
```

Ordinal Data

Ordinal data implies an ordering of the elements in a finite set (think "ordering" from the prefix "ord"). For example, there are different values for titles regarding software developers. As a simplified example, the set consisting of {D1, D2, SD1, SD2} can be used to specify junior developers (D1) up through senior developers (SD2), which have criteria associated with each level. Hence, integer-based and string-based elements of ordinal data are ordered.

Be careful with assumptions regarding integer-based ordinal data and relative values. For example, consider the following set of ordinal data S = {1,2,3,4,5,6} that represents grade levels in an organization. A level 2 employee is not "twice" as experienced as a level 1 employee, nor would a level 6 employee be three times as experienced as a level 2 (unless you define these values in such a manner).

Please read the `scikit-learn` documentation regarding the class `OrdinalEncoder` (`scikit-learn.preprocessing.OrdinalEncorder`) for handling ordinal data.

Categorical Data

Categorical data refers to nominal data as well as ordinal data: please read the preceding sections regarding the nuances involved in nominal data and ordinal data. Categorical data can only assume a finite set of distinct values, such as enumerations that are explained in a previous section. In addition, `Pandas` can explicitly specify a column as type categorical when you read the contents of a `CSV` file via the `read_csv()` method.

Interval Data

Interval data pertains to data that is ordered and lies in an interval or range, such as the integers and floating point numbers in the interval `[-1,1]`. Examples of interval data include temperature, income-versus-debt, and so forth. As you can see, interval data values can be negative as well as positive.

Ratio Data

Ratio data involves measured intervals, such as barometric pressure, height, altitude, and so forth. Notice the difference between interval data and ratio data: unlike interval data, ratio data *cannot* be negative. Obviously, it makes no sense to refer to negative barometric pressure, negative height, or negative altitude above the surface of the earth.

Continuous Data Versus Discrete Data

Continuous data can take on any value in an interval, such as `[-1,1]`, `[0,1]`, or `[5,10]`. Hence, continuous data involves floating point numbers, which includes interval data. Keep in mind that an interval contains an uncountably infinite number of values.

One other point to note pertains to possible values and their floating point representation. For instance, a random number in the interval `[0,1]` involves an uncountably infinite number of values, whereas its representation as a floating point number is limited to a large yet finite number of values. Let's suppose that N equals the integer 10^*1000 and it's the number of numbers in the interval `[0,1]` that can be represented as a floating point number. Then the smallest positive number in the interval `[0,1]` that can be represented as a floating point number is 1/N. However, there is an uncountably infinite number of values in the interval `[0,1/N)`, which we would assign a value (perhaps 0 or possibly 1/N).

Discrete data can take on a finite set of values, and the earlier comments regarding successors and predecessors apply to discrete data. As a simple example, the outcome of tossing a coin or throwing a die (or multiple dice) involves discrete data, which are also examples of nominal data. In addition, the associated probabilities for the outcomes form a discrete probability distribution (discussed later).

Qualitative and Quantitative Data

Quantitative data can be either discrete or continuous. For example, a person's age that is measured in years is discrete, whereas the height of a person is continuous. One point to keep in mind: the word "continuous" in statistics does not always have the same meaning when it's used in a mathematical context. For instance, the price of a house is treated as a continuous feature but it's not continuous in the mathematical sense because the smallest unit of measure is a penny, and there are many (in fact, an uncountably infinite number of) values between two consecutive penny values. Here are two examples of discrete data values, followed by three examples of continuous data values:

- revenue (money)
- number of items sold
- water temperature
- wind speed
- vehicle velocity

Each of the preceding data values are numeric types involving something that has business impact or has some physical characteristic.

Qualitative data can sometimes be represented as string-based values, such as different types of color or movie genres. Hence, nominal data and ordinal data are considered qualitative data.

As you saw in an earlier section, it's possible to use integer-based values for nominal values, such as days of the week, months of the year, and so forth. In fact, if a data set contains a string-based feature that is selected as input for a machine learning algorithm, those values are typically converted into integer based values, which can be performed via the `map()` function in `Pandas`. Here are additional examples of qualitative data:

- audio (length)
- pictures or paintings (dimensions)
- text (word count/file size)
- video (length)

Since the items in the preceding list have a parenthetical term that can be used to "measure" the various items, why are they not considered quantifiable and therefore measurable, just like the earlier bullet list? The key difference is that the items in the qualitative items are a form of multimedia, so they do not have a direct and immediate physical characteristic.

However, there are use cases in which media-related data *can* be treated as quantifiable. For example, suppose a company classifies ambient sounds. One practical scenario involves determining if a given sound is a gunshot versus the sound of a backfiring car. As such, the decibel level is an important quantifiable characteristic of both sounds.

In the case of paintings, it's certainly true that they can be "measured" by their selling price, which can sometimes be astronomical.

As another example, consider writers who are paid to write text-based documents. If their payment is based on the number of words in their documents, then the length of a document is a quantifiable characteristic.

On the other hand, people who read articles typically do not make a distinction between an article that contains 400 words, 450 words, or 500 words.

Finally, the cost of generating a text document that contains the dialogue in a movie can be affected by the length of the movie, in which case videos have a quantifiable characteristic.

Types of Statistical Data

The preceding sections described several data types, whereas this section classifies data types from a statistical standpoint. There are four primary types of statistical data, as shown below:

- nominal
- ordinal
- interval
- ratio

One way to remember these four types of statistical data is via the acronym NOIR (coincidentally the French word for "black"). Please refer to the earlier sections for details regarding any of these data types.

WORKING WITH DATA TYPES

If you have experience with programming languages, then you know that explicit data types exist (e.g., C, C++, Java, TypeScript, and so forth). Some programming languages, such as JavaScript and awk, do not require initializing variables with an explicit type: the type of a variable is inferred dynamically via an implicit type of system (i.e., one that is not directly exposed to a developer).

In machine learning, datasets can contain features that have different types of data, such as a combination of one or more of the following types of features:

- numeric data (integer/floating point and discrete/continuous)
- character/categorical data (different languages)
- date-related data (different formats)
- currency data (different formats)
- binary data (yes/no, 0/1, and so forth)
- nominal data (multiple unrelated values)
- ordinal data (multiple and related values)

Consider a dataset that contains real estate data, which can have 30 or more columns, often with the following features:

- the number of bedrooms in a house: a numeric value and a discrete value
- the number of square feet: a numeric value and (probably) a continuous value
- the name of the city: character data
- the construction date: a date value
- the selling price: a currency value and probably a continuous value
- the "for sale" status: binary data (either "yes" or "no")

An example of nominal data is the seasons in a year: although many countries have four distinct seasons, some countries have two distinct seasons. However, keep in mind that seasons can be associated with different temperature ranges (summer versus winter). An example of ordinal data is an employee pay grade: 1=entry level, 2=one year of experience, and so forth. Another example of nominal data is a set of colors, such as {Red, Green, Blue}.

A familiar example of binary data is the pair {Male, Female}, and some datasets contain a feature with these two values. If such a feature is required for training a model, first convert {Male, Female} to a numeric counterpart (such as {0,1}), and a `Pandas`-based example is here:

```
df['gender'] = df['gender'].map({'Male': 0,
'Female': 1})
```

Similarly, if you need to include a feature whose values are the previous set of colors, you can replace {Red, Green, Blue} with the values {0,1,2}. Categorical data is discussed in more detail later in this chapter.

WHAT IS DRIFT?

In machine learning terms, *drift* refers to any type of change in distribution over a period of time. *Model drift* refers to a change (drift) in the accuracy of a model's prediction, whereas *data drift* refers to a change in the type of data that is collected. Note that data drift is also called input drift, feature drift, or covariate drift.

There are several factors that influence the value of data, such as accuracy, relevance, and age. For example, physical stores that sell mobile phones are much more likely to sell recent phone models than older models. In some cases, data drift occurs over a period of time, and in other cases it's because some data is no longer relevant due to feature-related changes in an application. Always keep in mind that there might be multiple factors that can influence data drift in a specific dataset.

Two techniques for handling data drift are *domain classifier* and the *black-box shift detector*, both of which are discussed here:

https://blog.dataiku.com/towards-reliable-mlops-with-drift-detectors

In addition to the preceding types of drift, other types of changes can occur in a data set, some of which are listed below:

- concept shift
- covariate shift
- domain shift
- prior probability shift
- spurious correlation shift
- subpopulation shift
- time shift

Perform an online search to find more information about the topics in the preceding list of bullet items. Finally, the following list contains links to open-source `Python`-based tools that provide drift detection:

- alibi-detect (*https://github.com/SeldonIO/alibi-detect*)
- evidently (*https://github.com/evidentlyai/evidently*)

DISCRETE DATA VERSUS CONTINUOUS DATA

As a simple rule of thumb: *discrete* data involves a set of values that can be counted whereas continuous data must be measured. Discrete data can reasonably fit in a drop-down list of values, but there is no exact value for making such a determination. One person might think that a list of 500 values is discrete, whereas another person might think it's continuous.

For example, the list of provinces of Canada and the list of states of the USA are discrete data values, but is the same true for the number of countries in the world (roughly 200) or for the number of languages in the world (more than 7,000)?

On the other hand, values for temperature, humidity, and barometric pressure are considered *continuous* data types. Currency is also treated as continuous, even though there is a measurable difference between two consecutive values. The smallest unit of US currency is one penny, which is

1/100th of a dollar (accounting-based measurements use the "mil," which is 1/1,000th of a dollar).

Continuous data types can have subtle differences. For example, some-one who is 200 centimeters tall is twice as tall as someone who is 100 centimeters tall; similarly for 100 kilograms versus 50 kilograms. However, the temperature is different: 80 degrees Fahrenheit is not twice as hot as 40 degrees Fahrenheit.

Furthermore, keep in mind that the word "continuous" has a different meaning in mathematics and is not necessarily the same as continuous in machine learning. In the former, a continuous variable (let's say in the 2D Euclidean plane) can have an uncountably infinite number of values. On the other hand, a feature in a dataset that can have more values that can be "reasonably" displayed in a drop down list is treated *as though* it's a continuous variable.

For instance, values for stock prices are discrete: they must differ by at least a penny (or some other minimal unit of currency), which is to say, it's meaningless to say that the stock price changes by one-millionth of a penny. However, since there are "so many" possible stock values, it's treated as a continuous variable. The same comments apply to car mileage, ambient temperature, barometric pressure, and so forth.

"BINNING" DATA VALUES

The concept of "binning" refers to subdividing a set of values into multiple intervals, and then treating all the numbers in the same interval as though they had the same value. In addition, there are at least three techniques for binning data, as shown here:

- bins of equal widths
- bins of equal frequency
- bins based on k-means

More information about binning numerical features can be found here: *https://towardsdatascience.com/from-numerical-to-categorical-3252cf805ea2*

As a simple example of bins of equal widths, suppose that a feature in a dataset contains the age of people in a dataset. The range of values is approximately between 0 and 120, and we could "bin" them into 12 equal intervals, where each consists of 10 values: 0 through 9, 10 through 19, 20 through 29, and so forth.

As another example, using quartiles is even more coarse-grained than the earlier age-related binning example. The issue with binning pertains to the unintended consequences of classifying people in different bins, even though they are in close proximity to each other. For instance, some people struggle financially because they earn a meager wage, and they are also disqualified from financial assistance because their salary is higher than the cut-off point for receiving any assistance.

Scikit-learn provides the KBinsKDiscretizer class that uses a clustering algorithm for binning data:

https://scikit-learn.org/stable/modules/generated/sklearn.preprocessing. KBinsDiscretizer.html

In case you're interested, a highly technical paper (PDF) with information about clustering and binning can be accessed here:

https://www.stat.cmu.edu/tr/tr870/tr870.pdf

Programmatic Binning Techniques

Earlier in this chapter you saw a Pandas-based example of generating a histogram using data from a Titanic dataset. The number of bins was chosen on an *ad hoc* basis, with no relation to the data itself. However, there are several techniques that enable you to programmatically determine the optimal number of bins, some of which are shown as follows:

- Doane's formula
- Freedman–Diaconis' c hoice
- Rice's rule
- Scott's normal reference rule
- square-root choice
- Sturge's rule

Doane's formula for calculating the number of bins depends on the number of observations n and the kurtosis (discussed in Chapter 4) of the data, and it's reproduced here:

```
1 + log(n) + log(1 + kurtosis(data) * sqrt(n / 6.0))
```

Freedman–Diaconis' choice specifies the number of bins for a sample x, and it's based on the IQR (interquartile range) and the number of observations n, as shown in the following formula:

```
k = 2 * IRQ(x)/[cube root of n]
```

Sturge's rule to determine the number of bins k for Gaussian-based data is based on the number of observations n, and it's expressed as follows:

```
k = 1 + 3.322 * log n
```

In addition, after specifying the number of bins k, set the minimum bin width mbw as follows:

```
mbw = (Max Observed Value - Min Observed Value) / k
```

Experiment with the preceding formulas to determine which one provides the best visual display for your data. For more information about calculating the optimal number of bins, perform an online search for blog posts and articles.

Potential Issues When Binning Data Values

Partitioning the values of people's ages as described in the preceding section can be problematic. In particular, suppose that person A, person B, and person C are 29, 30, and 39, respectively. Then person A and person B are probably much more similar to each other than person B and person C, but because of the way in which the ages are partitioned, B is classified as closer to C than to A. In fact, binning can increase Type I errors (false positive) and Type II errors (false negative), as discussed in this blog post (along with some alternatives to binning):

https://medium.com/@peterflom/why-binning-continuous-data-is-almost-always-a-mistake-ad0b3a1d141f

CORRELATION

Correlation refers to the extent to which a pair of variables are related, which is a number between -1 and 1 inclusive. The most significant correlation values are -1, 0, and 1.

A correlation of 1 means that both variables increase and decrease in the same direction. A correlation of -1 means that both variables increase and decrease in the opposite direction. A correlation of 0 means that the variables are independent of each other.

Pandas provides the corr() method that generates a matrix containing the correlation between any pair of features in a data frame. Note that the diagonal values of this matrix are related to the variance of the features in the data frame.

A *correlation matrix* can be derived from a covariance matrix: each entry in the former matrix is a covariance value divided by the standard deviation of the two features in the row and column of a particular entry.

This concludes the portion of the chapter pertaining to dependencies among features in a dataset. The next section discusses different types of currencies that can appear in a dataset, along with a `Python` code sample for currency conversion.

What Is a Good Correlation Value?

Although there is no exact value that determines whether a correlation is weak, moderate, or strong, there are some guidelines, as shown here:

- `between 0.0 and 0.2: weak`
- `between 0.2 and 0.5: moderate`
- `between 0.5 and 0.7: moderately strong`
- `between 0.7 and 1.0: strong`

The preceding ranges are for positive correlations, and the corresponding values for negative correlations are shown here:

- `between -0.2 and 0:    weak`
- `between -0.5 and -0.2: moderate`
- `between -0.7 and -0.5: moderately strong`
- `between -0.7 and -1.0: strong`

However, treat the values in the preceding lists as guidelines: some people classify values between 0.0 and 0.4 as weak correlations, and values between 0.8 and 1.0 as strong correlations. In addition, a correlation of 0.0 means that there is no correlation at all (extra weak?).

Discrimination Threshold

Logistic regression (discussed in Chapter 6) is based on the sigmoid function (which in turn involves Euler's constant) whereby any real number is mapped to a number in the interval (0,1). Consequently, logistic regression is well-suited for classifying binary class membership: i.e., data points that belong to one of two classes. For datasets that contain two class values, let's call them 0 and 1, logistic regression provides a probability that a data point belongs to class 1 or class 1, where the range of probability values includes all the numbers in the interval [0,1].

The *discrimination threshold* is the value whereby larger probabilities are associated with class 1 and smaller probabilities are associated with class 0. Some datasets have a discrimination threshold of 0.5, but in general, this value can be much closer to 0 or 1. Relevant examples include health-related datasets (healthy versus cancer), sports events (win versus lose), and even the DMV (department of motor vehicles), where the latter require 85% accuracy in order to pass the test in some US states.

WORKING WITH SYNTHETIC DATA

The ability to generate synthetic data—also called fake data—has practical uses, particularly in imbalanced datasets. Sometimes it's necessary to generate synthetic data that closely approximates legitimate data because it's not possible to obtain actual data values.

For example, suppose that a dataset contains 1,000 rows of patient data in which fifty people have cancer and 950 people are healthy. This dataset is obviously imbalanced, and from a human standpoint, you *want* this dataset to be imbalanced (you want everyone to be healthy). Unfortunately, machine learning algorithms can be affected by imbalanced datasets whereby they can "favor" the class that has more values (i.e., healthy individuals). There are several ways to mitigate the effect of imbalanced datasets, which is described in Chapter 2.

In the meantime, let's delve into the `Python`-based open-source library `Faker` for generating synthetic data, as discussed in the next section.

What Is Faker?

The open source `Python` library `Faker` is a very easy-to-use library that enables you to generate synthetic data, and its home page is here:

https://pypi.org/project/Faker/

On your machine, open a command shell and launch the following command:

```
pip3 install faker
```

After successfully installing `faker`, you're ready to generate a dataset with synthetic data.

A Python Code Sample With Faker

If you have not already installed the `Python` library `Faker` on your machine, open a command shell and launch the following command:

```
pip3 install faker
```

After successfully installing `faker`, you're ready to generate synthetic data. For example, Listing 1.1 displays the contents of `faker1.py` that generates a synthetic name.

Listing 1.1: faker1.py

```
import faker

fake = faker.Faker()

name = fake.name()
print("fake name:",name)
```

Open a command shell and navigate to the directory that contains the file `faker1.py` and launch the code with the following command:

```
python faker1.py
```

You will see the following output:

```
fake name: Dr. Laura Moore
```

Launching Faker From the Command Line

The previous section showed you a `Python` code sample for generating a synthetic name, and this section shows you how to generate synthetic values from the command line. Navigate to a command shell and type the following command to generate a synthetic name (lines that start with a "$" indicates commands for you to type):

```
$ faker address
96060 Hall Ridge Apt. 662
Brianton, IN 19597

$ faker address
8881 Amber Center Apt. 410
New Jameston, AZ 47448
```

```
$ faker name

Jessica Harvey
$ faker email
ray14@example.org

$ faker zipcode
45863

$ faker state
South Dakota

$ faker city
Sierrachester
```

As you can see, `Faker` generates different values for addresses, and similarly for other features (e.g., name, email, and so forth). The next section shows you a systematic way to generate synthetic data and then see that data to a CSV file.

Generating and Saving Customer Data

Listing 1.2 displays the contents of `gen_customers.py` TBD that generates a set of customer names and saves them to a CSV file.

Listing 1.2: gen_customers.py

```python
import os

# make sure we have an empty CSV file:
if os.path.exists(filename):
  os.remove(filename)
else:
  print("File "+filename+" does not exist")

import pandas as pd
import faker
```

```
fake = faker.Faker()

# the name of the CSV file with customer data:
filename = "fake_customers.csv"

customer_ids = [100,200,300,400]

###############################################
# 1) loop through values in customer_ids
# 2) generate a customer record
# 3) append the record to the CSV file
###############################################

for cid in customer_ids:
  customer = [
     {
        "cust_id": cid,
        "name": fake.name(),
        "address": fake.street_address(),
        "email": fake.email()
     }
  ]

  # create a Pandas data frame with the customer
record:
  df = pd.DataFrame(data = customer )

  # append the generated customer record to the CSV
file:
  df.to_csv(filename, mode='a', index=False,
header=False)
```

Listing 1.2 starts by assigning a value to the variable filename, followed by a conditional block that checks whether or not the file already exists, in which case the file is removed from the file system. The next section contains several `import` statements, followed by initializing the variable `fake` as an instance of the `Faker` class.

The next section initializes the variable `customer_ids` with values for four customers, followed by a loop that iterates through the values in the `customer_ids`. During each iteration, the code creates a customer record that contains four attributes:

- a customer ID (obtained from customer_ids)
- a synthetic name
- a synthetic street address
- a synthetic email address

The next portion of Listing 1.1 create a `Pandas` data frame called `df` that is initialized with the contents of the customer record, after which the data frame contents are appended to the `CSV` file that is specified near the beginning of Listing 1.1. Now launch the code in Listing 1.1 by typing python `gen_customers.py` from the command line and you will see the following type of output, which will be similar to (but different from) the output on your screen:

```
100,Jaime Peterson,17228 Kelli Cliffs Apt.
625,clinejohnathan@hotmail.com
200,Mark Smith,729 Cassandra Isle Apt. 768,brandon36@
hotmail.com
300,Patrick Pacheco,84460 Griffith Loaf,charles61@
proctor.com
400,Justin Owens,2221 Renee Villages,kyates@myers.com
```

Use the contents of Listing 1.2 as a template for your own data requirements, which involves changing the field types and the output `CSV` file.

The next section shows you a Python code sample that uses the `Faker` library in order to generate a `CSV` file called `fake_purch_orders.csv` that contains synthetic purchase orders for each customer ID that is specified in Listing 1.2.

Generating Purchase Orders (Optional)

This section is marked optional because it's useful only if you need to generate synthetic data that is associated with data in another dataset. After customers register themselves in an application, they can have one or more associated purchase orders, where each purchase order is identified by the ID of the customer and an ID for the purchase order row.

Listing 1.3 displays the contents of gen_purch_orders.py that shows you how to generate synthetic purchase orders for the list of customers in Listing 1.2 using the Faker library.

Listing 1.3: gen_purch_orders.py

```
filename = "fake_purch_orders.csv"

import os
if os.path.exists(filename):
  os.remove(filename)
else:
  print("File "+filename+" does not exist")

import pandas as pd
import numpy as np
import random
import faker

fake = faker.Faker()

#########################
# hard-coded values for:
# customers
# purchase orders ids
# purchased item  ids
#########################

customer_ids = [100,200,300,400]
purch_orders = [1100,1200,1300,1400]
item_ids     = [510,511,512]

outer_counter=1
outer_offset=0
outer_increment = 1000
```

```
inner_counter=1
inner_offset=0
inner_increment = 10

for cid in customer_ids:
  pid_outer_offset = outer_counter*outer_increment
  for pid in purch_orders:
    purch_inner_offset = pid_outer_offset+inner_
counter*inner_increment
    for item_id in item_ids:
      purch_order = [
        {
          "cust_id": cid,
          "purch_id": purch_inner_offset,
          "item_id": item_id,
        }
      ]
      df = pd.DataFrame(data = purch_order)
      df.to_csv(filename, mode='a', index=False,
header=False)
    inner_counter += 1
  outer_counter += 1
```

Listing 1.3 starts with code that is similar to Listing 1.2, followed by a code block that initializes the values for the variables `customer_ids`, `purch_orders`, and `item_ids` that represent `id` values for customers, purchase orders, and purchased_items, respectively. Keep in mind that these variables contain hard-coded values: in general, an application generates the values for customers and for their purchase orders.

The next portion of Listing 1.3 is a nested loop whose outer loop iterates through the values in the variable customer_ids, and for each ID, an inner loop iterates through the values in the variable `purch_orders`. Yet another nested loop iterates through the values in the `item_ids` variable.

One point to keep in mind that the underlying assumption in this code sample is that every purchase order for every customer contains purchases for every item, which in general is not the case. However, the purpose of this code sample is to generate synthetic data, which is not required to be identical to customer purchasing patterns. Fortunately, it *is* possible to modify the code in Listing 1.3 so that purchase orders contain a randomly selected subset of items, in case you need that level of randomness in the generated CSV file.

The remaining portion of Listing 1.3 works in the same manner as the corresponding code in Listing 1.2: each time a new purchase order is generated, a data frame is populated with the data in the purchase order, after which the contents of the data frame are appended to the CSV file that is specified near the beginning of Listing 1.3. Launch the code in Listing 1.2 and you will see the following type of output:

```
100,1010,510
100,1010,511
100,1010,512
100,1020,510
100,1020,511
100,1020,512
100,1030,510
100,1030,511
100,1030,512
100,1040,510
100,1040,511
100,1040,512
//details omitted for brevity
400,4130,510
400,4130,511
400,4130,512
400,4140,510
400,4140,511
400,4140,512
400,4150,510
400,4150,511
400,4150,512
400,4160,510
400,4160,511
400,4160,512
```

Listing 1.4 is similar to the earlier code samples: the difference is that this code sample generates synthetic data for item descriptions. Now launch the code in Listing 1.4 and you will see the following

SUMMARY

This chapter started with a brief description of data literacy as well as some aspects of `EDA` (exploratory data analysis).

Then you learned about common types of data, such a binary, nominal, ordinal, and categorical data. You were also instructed about continuous versus discrete data, quantitative and quantitative data, and types of statistical data.

In addition, you were taught about concepts such as data drift and data leakage. Next you learned about processing categorical data and how to map categorical data to numeric data. Finally, you learned how to use the Python-based library called Faker in order to generate datasets containing synthetic data.

REFERENCES

Wikipedia. 2022. *Data quality.* https://en.wikipedia.org/wiki/Data_quality. Last updated June 28 2022.

Wikipedia. 2023. *Data literacy.* https://en.wikipedia.org/wiki/Data_literacy. Last updated May 9, 2023.

OUTLIER AND ANOMALY DETECTION

This chapter shows you how to process outliers, anomalies, and missing data, as well as data cleaning and data wrangling techniques. In addition, this chapter includes short (i.e., half a page or less) `Python` code samples that use `NumPy` as well as `Pandas` to find outliers, how to calculate z-scores, and how to count the number of missing values in a dataset.

The first part of this chapter discusses the relationship among fraud, anomalies, and outliers, along with `Python` code samples that illustrate how to find outliers. The second section discusses fraud detection (there are many types), along with anomaly detection. The third section contains details regarding the bias-variance tradeoff and various types of statistical bias.

WORKING WITH OUTLIERS

In brief, an *outlier* is an abnormal data value that is outside the range of "normal" values in a dataset. For example, a person's height in centimeters is typically between 30 centimeters and 250 centimeters, which means that a height of 5 centimeters or a height of 500 centimeters is an outlier because those values are not possible for humans.

Outliers in a dataset are significantly larger or smaller than the inliers in a data set. Outliers exist for various reasons, such as data variability, experimental errors, or erroneous measurements. In addition, outliers can create issues during statistical analysis, such as adversely affecting the value of the mean and the standard deviation. Three types of outliers are explained here:

https://pub.towardsai.net/the-7-stages-of-preparing-data-for-machine-learning-dfe454da960b

Outlier Detection/Removal

There are techniques available that help you detect outliers in a dataset, as shown in the following bullet list, along with a one-line description and links for additional information:

- IQR
- z-score
- trimming
- winsoring
- minimum covariance determinant
- local outlier factor
- Huber and Ridge
- isolation forest (tree-based algorithm)
- one-class SVM

The IQR (interquantile range) algorithm detects data points that are outside of 1.5 times of an interquartile range that either lie above the 3rd quartile or lie below the 1st quartile. Such points can be considered outliers.

The *z-score* for data points involves subtracting the mean and then dividing by the standard deviation:

```
Z-score = (X-mean)/std
```

In general, z-scores that are greater than 3 are considered outliers, but you can adjust this value (e.g., 2.5 or 2) that is more suitable for your dataset.

Perhaps *trimming* is the simplest technique (apart from dropping outliers), which involves removing rows whose feature value is in the upper 5% range or the lower 5% range. *Winsorizing* the data is an improvement over trimming: set the values in the top 5% range equal to the maximum value in the 95th percentile, and set the values in the bottom 5% range equal to the minimum in the 5th percentile.

The *minimum covariance determinant* is a covariance-based technique, and a `Python`-based code sample that uses this technique is downloadable here:

https://scikit-learn.org/stable/modules/outlier_detection.html

Two other techniques involve the *Huber* and the *Ridge* classes, both of which are included as part of `Scikit-learn`. `Huber` error is less sensitive to outliers because it's calculated via linear loss, similar to **MAE** (mean absolute error). A code sample that compares `Huber` and `Ridge` is downloadable here:

https://scikit-learn.org/stable/auto_examples/linear_model/plot_huber_vs_ridge.html

You can also explore the Theil-Sen estimator and RANSAC that are "robust" against outliers, and additional information is here:

https://scikit-learn.org/stable/auto_examples/linear_model/plot_theilsen. html

https://en.wikipedia.org/wiki/Random_sample_consensus

Four algorithms for outlier detection are discussed here:

https://www.kdnuggets.com/2018/12/four-techniques-outlier-detection. html

One other scenario involves "local" outliers. For example, suppose that you use kMeans (or some other clustering algorithm) and determine that a value is an outlier with respect to one of the clusters. While this value is not necessarily an "absolute" outlier, detecting such a value might be important for your use case.

Incorrectly Scaled Values Versus Outliers

You already know that an outlier is a value that is significantly different from the other values for a given feature. Now suppose that a numeric feature has a set of values in the range [90,100], but the correct range of values for this feature is [9,10]. Notice that the incorrect values do not contain any outliers, and also that those values can easily be scaled the range [0,1] using a technique described in Chapter 1.

However, suppose that you are not a domain expert for the data in this dataset, so you do not realize that the initial values are out of range for that feature. As a result, you proceed to scale these data values so that they are in the range [0,1]. Although it's possible to train a model with this scaled dataset, the newly scaled values (as well as the initial values) are incorrect. Unfortunately, errors can arise when you perform other operations with this data, such as calculating the correlation between this feature and some other feature in the dataset. Hence, it's important to have domain knowledge in order to detect and rectify this type of error.

Other Outlier Techniques

If you want to explore additional techniques for detecting outliers, the following technicals are also available:

- modified z-score
- MAD (median absolute deviation)

- Tukey's box plot
- Carling median rule

In brief, the modified z-score provides a more fine-trained set of values that sometimes detect outliers that are not detected via a standard z-score. The MAD technique uses a median-based technique (instead of mean and variance values) that is less sensitive to outliers, which is better suited for non-normal distributions. Tukey's boxplot uses quartile values, whereas the Carling median rule uses median values. Perform an online search for more details, formulas, and code samples regarding the outlier techniques in the preceding bullet list.

FINDING OUTLIERS WITH NUMPY

Although we have not discussed the NumPy library, we will only use the NumPy array() method, the mean() method, and the std() method in this section, all of which have intuitive functionality.

Listing 2.1 displays the contents of numpy_outliers1.py that illustrates how to use NumPy methods to find outliers in an array of numbers.

Listing 2.1: numpy_outliers1.py

```python
import numpy as np

arr1 = np.array([2,5,7,9,9,40])
print("values:",arr1)

data_mean = np.mean(arr1)
data_std  = np.std(arr1)
print("data_mean:",data_mean)
print("data_std:" ,data_std)
print()

multiplier = 1.5
cut_off = data_std * multiplier
lower = data_mean - cut_off
upper = data_mean + cut_off
print("lower cutoff:",lower)
```

```
print("upper cutoff:",upper)
print()


outliers = [x for x in arr1 if x < lower or x > upper]
print('Identified outliers: %d' % len(outliers))
print("outliers:",outliers)
```

Listing 2.1 starts by defining a `NumPy` array of numbers and then calculates the mean and standard deviation of those numbers. The next block of code initializes two numbers that represent the upper and lower values that are based on the value of the cut_off variable. Any numbers in the array `arr1` that lie to the left of the lower value or to the right of the upper value are treated as outliers.

The final section of code in Listing 2.1 initializes the variable `outliers` with the numbers that are determined to be outliers, and those values are printed. Launch the code in Listing 2.1 and you will see the following output:

```
values: [ 2  5  7  9  9 40]
data_mean: 12.0
data_std: 12.754084313139327


lower cutoff: -7.131126469708988
upper cutoff: 31.13112646970899


Identified outliers: 1
outliers: [40]
```

The preceding code sample specifies a hard-coded value in order to calculate the upper and lower range values.

Listing 2.2 is an improvement in that you can specify a set of values from which to calculate the upper and lower range values, and the new block of code is shown in bold.

Listing 2.2: numpy_outliers2.py

```
import numpy as np


arr1 = np.array([2,5,7,9,9,40])
print("values:",arr1)
```

```
data_mean = np.mean(arr1)
data_std  = np.std(arr1)
print("data_mean:",data_mean)
print("data_std:" ,data_std)
print()


multipliers = np.array([0.5,1.0,1.5,2.0,2.5,3.0])
for multiplier in multipliers:
   cut_off = data_std * multiplier
   lower, upper = data_mean - cut_off, data_mean + cut_
off
   print("=> multiplier:  ",multiplier)
   print("lower cutoff:",lower)
   print("upper cutoff:",upper)


   outliers = [x for x in df['data'] if x < lower or x >
upper]
   print('Identified outliers: %d' % len(outliers))
   print("outliers:",outliers)
   print()
```

Listing 2.2 contains a block of new code that initializes the variable multipliers as an array of numeric values that are used for finding outliers. Although you will probably use a value of 2.0 or larger on a real dataset, this range of numbers can give you a better sense of detecting outliers. Now launch the code in Listing 2.2 and you will see the following output:

```
values: [ 2   5   7   9   9  40]
data_mean: 12.0
data_std: 12.754084313139327

lower cutoff: -7.131126469708988
upper cutoff: 31.13112646970899

Identified outliers: 1
outliers: [40]
=> multiplier:   0.5
```

```
lower cutoff: 5.622957843430337
upper cutoff: 18.377042156569665
Identified outliers: 3
outliers: [2, 5, 40]

=> multiplier:   1.0
lower cutoff: -0.7540843131393267
upper cutoff: 24.754084313139327
Identified outliers: 1
outliers: [40]

=> multiplier:   1.5
lower cutoff: -7.131126469708988
upper cutoff: 31.13112646970899
Identified outliers: 1
outliers: [40]

=> multiplier:   2.0
lower cutoff: -13.508168626278653
upper cutoff: 37.50816862627865
Identified outliers: 1
outliers: [40]

=> multiplier:   2.5
lower cutoff: -19.88521078284832
upper cutoff: 43.88521078284832
Identified outliers: 0
outliers: []

=> multiplier:   3.0
lower cutoff: -26.262252939417976
upper cutoff: 50.26225293941798
Identified outliers: 0
outliers: []
```

FINDING OUTLIERS WITH PANDAS

The `Pandas` code sample in this section involves a very simple `Pandas` data frame, the `mean()` method, and the `std()` method.

Listing 2.3 displays the contents of `pandas_outliers1.py` that illustrates how to use `Pandas` to find outliers in an array of numbers.

Listing 2.3: pandas_outliers1.py

```python
import pandas as pd

df = pd.DataFrame([2,5,7,9,9,40])
df.columns = ["data"]

print("=> complete data set:")
print(df)
print()

data_mean = df['data'].mean()
data_std  = df['data'].std()
print("=> data_mean:",data_mean)
print("=> data_std: ",data_std)
print()

multiplier = 1.5
cut_off = data_std * multiplier
lower, upper = data_mean - cut_off, data_mean + cut_off
print("=> lower cutoff:",lower)
print("=> upper cutoff:",upper)
print()

# outliers: method #1
outliers = [x for x in df['data'] if x < lower or x >
upper]
print('=> Identified outliers: %d' % len(outliers))
print("=> outliers (#1):",outliers)
print()
```

```
# outliers: method #2
outliers = [x for x in df['data'] if x < lower or x >
upper]
outliers = df[(df.data < lower) | (df.data > upper)]
print('=> Identified outliers: %d' % len(outliers))
print("=> outliers (#2):",outliers)
print()

# keep the inliers and drop the outliers:
df = df[(df.data > lower) & (df.data < upper)]
print("=> inliers without outliers:")
print(df)
print()
```

Listing 2.3 starts by defining a `Pandas` data frame and then calculates the mean and standard deviation of those numbers. The next block of code initializes two numbers that represent the upper and lower values that are based on the value of the `cut_off` variable. Any numbers in the data frame that lie to the left of the lower value or to the right of the upper value are treated as outliers.

The final section of code in Listing 2.3 initializes the variable `outliers` with the numbers that are determined to be outliers by means of a `Python` comprehension, and those values are printed, whereas the second technique accomplishes the same result without a `Python` comprehension. Launch the code in Listing 2.3 and you will see the following output:

```
=> complete data set:
   data
0    2
1    5
2    7
3    9
4    9
5    40

=> data_mean:  12.0
=> data_std:   13.971399357258385
```

```
=> lower cutoff: -8.957099035887577
=> upper cutoff: 32.95709903588758

=> Identified outliers: 1
=> outliers (#1): [40]

=> Identified outliers: 1
=> outliers (#2):     data
5      40

=> inliers without outliers:
    data
0      2
1      5
2      7
3      9
4      9
```

The preceding code sample specifies a hard-coded value in order to calculate the upper and lower range values.

Listing 2.4 is an improvement over Listing 2.3 in that you can specify a set of values from which to calculate the upper and lower range values, and the new block of code is shown in bold.

Listing 2.4: pandas_outliers2.py

```
import pandas as pd

#df = pd.DataFrame([2,5,7,9,9,40])
#df = pd.DataFrame([2,5,7,8,42,44])

df = pd.DataFrame([2,5,7,8,42,492])
df.columns = ["data"]
print("=> data values:")
print(df['data'])
```

```
data_mean = df['data'].mean()
data_std  = df['data'].std()
print("=> data_mean:",data_mean)
print("=> data_std:" ,data_std)
print()

multipliers = [0.5,1.0,1.5,2.0,2.5,3.0]
for multiplier in multipliers:
  cut_off = data_std * multiplier
  lower, upper = data_mean - cut_off, data_mean + cut_
off
  print("=> multiplier:   ",multiplier)
  print("lower cutoff:",lower)
  print("upper cutoff:",upper)

  outliers = [x for x in df['data'] if x < lower or x >
upper]
  print('Identified outliers: %d' % len(outliers))
  print("outliers:",outliers)
  print()
```

Listing 2.4 contains a block of new code that initializes the variable `mul-tipliers` as an array of numeric values that are used for finding outliers. Although you will probably use a value of 2.0 or larger on a real dataset, this range of numbers can give you a better sense of detecting outliers. Now launch the code in Listing 2.4 and you will see the following output:

```
=> data values:
0      2
1      5
2      7
3      8
4     42
5    492
Name: data, dtype: int64
=> data_mean: 92.66666666666667
=> data_std: 196.187325448579
```

```
=> multiplier:    0.5
lower cutoff: -5.42699605762283
upper cutoff: 190.76032939095617
Identified outliers: 1
outliers: [492]

=> multiplier:    1.0
lower cutoff: -103.52065878191233
upper cutoff: 288.85399211524566
Identified outliers: 1
outliers: [492]

=> multiplier:    1.5
lower cutoff: -201.6143215062018
upper cutoff: 386.9476548395352
Identified outliers: 1
outliers: [492]

=> multiplier:    2.0
lower cutoff: -299.7079842304913
upper cutoff: 485.0413175638247
Identified outliers: 1
outliers: [492]

=> multiplier:    2.5
lower cutoff: -397.80164695478084
upper cutoff: 583.1349802881142
Identified outliers: 0
outliers: []

=> multiplier:    3.0
lower cutoff: -495.8953096790703
upper cutoff: 681.2286430124036
Identified outliers: 0
outliers: []
```

Calculating Z-Scores to Find Outliers

The z-score of a set of numbers is calculated by standardizing those numbers, which involves 1) subtracting their mean from each number, and 2) dividing by their standard deviation. Although you can perform these steps manually, the Python SciPy library simplifies the steps involved. If need be, you can install this package with the following command:

```
pip3 install scipy
```

Listing 2.5 displays the contents of outliers_zscores.py that illustrates how to find outliers in an array of numbers. As you will see, this code sample relies on convenience methods from Numpy, Pandas, and SciPy.

Listing 2.5: outliers_zscores.py

```
import numpy as np
import pandas as pd
from scipy import stats

arr1 = np.array([2,5,7,9,9,40])
print("values:",arr1)


df = pd.DataFrame(arr1)

zscores = np.abs(stats.zscore(df))
print("z scores:")
print(zscores)
print()


upper = 2.0
lower = 0.5
print("=> upper outliers:")
print(zscores[np.where(zscores > upper)])
print()

print("=> lower outliers:")
print(zscores[np.where(zscores < lower)])
print()
```

Listing 2.5 starts with several `import` statements, followed by initializing the variable `arr1` as a `Numpy` array of numbers, and then displaying the values in `arr1`. The next code snippet initializes the variable `df` as a data frame that contains the values in the variable `arr1`.

Next, the variable `zscores` is initialized with the z-scores of the elements of the df data frame, as shown here:

```
zscores = np.abs(stats.zscore(df))
```

The next section of code initializes the variables `upper` and `lower`, and the z-scores whose values are less than the value of `lower` or greater than the value `upper` are treated as outliers, and those values are displayed. Launch the code in Listing 2.5 and you will see the following output:

```
values: [ 2   5   7   9   9  40]
z scores:
[[0.78406256]
 [0.54884379]
 [0.39203128]
 [0.23521877]
 [0.23521877]
 [2.19537517]]

=> upper outliers:
[2.19537517]

=> lower outliers:
[0.39203128 0.23521877 0.23521877]
```

FRAUD DETECTION

According to one estimate, worldwide fraud amounts to more than five trillion dollars. You can read the article here: *https://www.crowe.com/global/news/fraud-costs-the-global-economy-over-us$5-trillion*

Earlier sections in this chapter discussed how outliers differ from inliers in terms of their value, frequency, or location, or some combination. On the other hand, inliers are common occurrences, which is to say, there is nothing unusual about the values for inliers. An outlier draws attention to the possibility of fraud but does not necessarily indicate that fraud has occurred.

An *anomaly* is also an outlier that is a more serious type of outlier: there is a greater chance that this type of outlier is also fraud. By way of analogy, consider a traffic light consisting of green (go), yellow (caution), and red (stop). An outlier can be in any of the following ranges:

*   between green and red
*   between green and yellow
*   between yellow and red

As such, there are different levels of caution involved with anomalies and outliers. Specifically, an anomaly belongs to the third category, whereas a "benign" outlier (which is *not* an anomaly) is in the second category. Moreover, the collection of all types of outliers is in the first category. With the preceding points in mind, here is a short list of various types of fraud:

*   credit card fraud
*   payroll fraud
*   insurance fraud

Although there is no single method for always determining fraud, there are some techniques for detecting potentially fraudulent transactions. For example, if you encounter a suspicious event for a customer, calculate the following values for that customer:

*   total purchase amount for this day
*   number of transactions for this day
*   time of day for each transaction
*   number of locations
*   addresses of those locations

Now compare the values in the preceding list with the customer daily transaction patterns to see if there is a likely case of fraud. In case you're interested, the following link contains a list of 41 types of fraud, along with techniques for fraud prevention:

https://www.i-sight.com/resources/41-types-of-fraud-and-how-to-detect-and-prevent-them/

TECHNIQUES FOR ANOMALY DETECTION

First, let's keep in mind that an anomaly is also an outlier: the difference is that the consequences of an anomaly can be much worse than an outlier. For example, consider credit card purchases whereby a person who living in San Francisco suddenly makes credit card purchases in New York City. A one-time purchase could be an anomaly (i.e., a stolen credit card), or it would be purchased during a short stop-over en route to a vacation in another city or country (i.e., a type 1 error). A business trip or a vacation in New York City would probably involve a larger set of credit card purchases, and therefore normal purchases instead of credit card theft.

Consider a variation of the preceding scenario: a customer on a business trip in New York City has his credit card stolen and then multiple credit card purchases are made in San Francisco. The latter might escape detection because the customer lives in San Francisco (i.e., a type 2 error). However, if multiple credit card purchases are made simultaneously in San Francisco and New York City during the same period of time, there is a greater risk of anomalous behavior because a spouse making credit card purchases with a card that is linked to the same bank account would have a different credit card number.

Incidentally, credit card companies *do* provide a telephone menu option to "notify us of any upcoming business or travel plans," which can help reduce the possibility of type 1 or type 2 errors associated with credit card purchases.

In addition to credit card fraud, there are many other types of fraud, such as insurance fraud and or payroll fraud. In fact, the following link contains an assortment of 41 types of fraud, along with short descriptions of each type:

https://www.i-sight.com/resources/41-types-of-fraud-and-how-to-detect-and-prevent-them/

Before we explore this topic, it's worth noting that various types of machine learning algorithms are available for detecting anomalies. One type involves classification algorithms, such as kNN, decision trees, and SVMs. Another type involves unsupervised algorithms, such as autoencoders (a deep learning architecture), GMM (Gaussian mixture models), kMeans (a well-known clustering algorithm), and PCA (discussed in Chapter 6).

However, since this book is not primarily about machine learning or deep learning algorithms, this chapter discusses other techniques for anomaly detection. Note that kNN is discussed later in this chapter, and decision trees are relevant to entropy and `Gini` impurity (discussed in Chapter 5).

One other technique for anomaly detection uses a Bayesian network, which is a probabilistic graphical model (PGM). Bayesian networks and PGMs are outside the scope of this book, but the following link contains information about anomaly detection using a Bayesian network:

https://www.bayesserver.com/docs/techniques/anomaly-detection

Selecting an Anomaly Detection Technique

Unfortunately, there is no simple way to *decide* how to deal with anomalies and outliers in a dataset. Although you can drop rows that contain outliers, keep in mind that doing so might deprive the dataset – and therefore the trained model - of valuable information. You can try modifying the data values (described below), but again, this might lead to erroneous inferences in the trained model.

Another possibility is to train a model with the dataset that contains anomalies and outliers, and then train a model with a dataset from which the anomalies and outliers have been removed. Compare the two results and see if you can infer anything meaningful regarding the anomalies and outliers. Various techniques are available for anomaly detection, some of which are listed below:

- LOF
- HBOS
- PyOD
- Numeric Outlier (IQR)
- Z-Score
- DBSCAN
- Isolation Forest

Perform an online search for articles that discuss deep learning and anomaly detection, as well as the products that are in the preceding bullet list.

WORKING WITH IMBALANCED DATASETS

Imbalanced datasets contain at least once class that has significantly more values than another class in the dataset. For example, if class A has 99% of the data and class B has 1%, which classification algorithm would you use?

Unfortunately, classification algorithms don't work as well with highly imbalanced datasets. However, there are various techniques that you can use in order to reduce the imbalance in a dataset. Regardless of the technique that you decide to use, keep in mind the following detail: *resampling techniques are only applied to the training data* (not the validation data or the test data).

In addition, if you perform k-fold cross validation on a training set, then oversampling is performed in each fold during the training step. In order to avoid data leakage, make sure that you do *not* perform oversampling prior to k-fold cross validation.

Data Sampling Techniques

Data sampling techniques reduce the imbalance in an imbalanced datasets, and some well-known techniques are listed below:

- random resampling: rebalances the class distribution
- random undersampling: deletes examples from the majority class
- random oversampling: duplicates data in the minority class
- SMOTE (synthetic minority oversampling technique)

Random resampling rebalances the class distribution by resampling the data space in order to reduce the discrepancy between the number of rows in the majority class and the minority class.

On the other hand, the *random undersampling* technique removes samples that belong to the majority class from the dataset, and involves the following:

- randomly remove samples from majority class
- can be performed with or without replacement
- alleviates imbalance in the dataset
- may increase the variance of the classifier
- may discard useful or important samples

However, random undersampling does not work so well with extremely unbalanced datasets, such as a 99% and 1% split into two classes. Moreover, undersampling can result in losing information that is useful for a model.

Random oversampling generates new samples from a minority class: this technique duplicates examples from the minority class.

Another option to consider is the `Python` package `imbalanced-learn` in the `scikit-learn-contrib` project. This project provides various resampling techniques for datasets that exhibit class imbalance. More details are here:

https://github.com/scikit-learn-contrib/imbalanced-learn

Another well-known technique is called SMOTE, which involves data augmentation (i.e., synthesizing new data samples). SMOTE was initially developed by means of the kNN algorithm (other options are available), and it can be an effective technique for handling imbalanced classes. SMOTE is not discussed in this chapter, but you can find free online articles that describe SMOTE.

Removing Noisy Data

There are several techniques that attempt to remove so-called noisy data, which is often near the boundary, so that there is less ambiguity in the classification of the remaining data. Some of these techniques are listed here:

- near miss
- CNN (condensed nearest neighbor)
- Tomek links
- ENN (edited nearest neighbor)
- OSS (one-sided selection)
- NCR neighborhood cleaning rule

SUMMARY

This chapter started with a discussion regarding the relationship among fraud, anomalies, and outliers, along with `Python` code samples that illustrate how to find outliers. The second section discusses fraud detection (there are many types), along with anomaly detection. Next, you learned about algorithms such as `SMOTE` for handling imbalanced classes in a dataset. Finally, you learned about the bias-variance tradeoff and various types of statistical bias.

## CHAPTER 3

CLEANING DATASETS

This chapter shows you how to clean datasets, which includes finding missing data, incorrect data, and duplicate data. In some cases you might also decide to consolidate data values (e.g., treat the prefix Mr, MR, and mr as the same label).

The first part of this chapter contains several `Pandas` code samples that use `Pandas` to read `CSV` files and then calculate statistical values such as the mean, median, mode, and standard deviation.

The second part of this chapter uses `Pandas` to handle missing values in `CSV` files, starting with `CSV` files that contain a single column, followed by two-column `CSV` files. These code samples will prepare you to work with multi-column `CSV` files, such as the Titanic `titanic.csv` `CSV` file.

ANALYZING MISSING DATA

This section contains subsections that describes types of missing data, common causes of missing data, and various ways to input values for missing data. Keep in mind that outlier detection, fraud detection, and anomaly detection pertain to analyzing *existing* data.

By contrast, missing data presents a different issue, which in turn raises the following question: what can you do about the missing values? Is it better to discard data points (e.g., rows in a `CSV` file) with missing values, or is it better to estimate reasonable values as a replacement for the missing values? Also keep in mind that missing data can adversely affect a thorough analysis of a dataset, whereas erroneous data can increase bias and uncertainty.

At this point you've undoubtedly realized that a single solution does not exist for every dataset: you need to perform an analysis on a case-by-case basis, after you have learned some of the techniques that might help you effectively address missing data values.

Causes of Missing Data

There are various reasons for missing values in a dataset, some of which are listed here:

- values are unavailable
- values were improperly collected
- inaccurate data entry

Although you might be tempted to *always* replace a missing values with a concrete value, there are situations in which you cannot determine a value. As a simple example, a survey that contains questions for people under 30 will have a missing value for respondents who are over 30, and in this case specifying a value for the missing value would be incorrect. With these details in mind, there are various ways to fill missing values, some of which are listed here:

- remove rows with a high percentage of missing values (50% or larger)
- one-hot encoding for categorical data
- handling data inconsistency
- use the Imputer class from scikit-learn library
- fill missing values with the values in an adjacent row
- replace missing data with the mean/median/mode value
- infer ("impute") the value for missing data

Once again, the technique that you select for filling missing values is influenced by various factors, such as:

- how you want to process the data
- the type of data involved
- the cause of missing values (see first list in this section)

Although the most common technique involves the mean value for numeric features, someone needs to determine which technique is appropriate for a given feature.

However, if you are not confident that you can impute a reasonable value, consider deleting the row with a missing value, and then train a model with the imputed value and also with the deleted row.

One problem that can arise after removing rows with missing values is that the resulting dataset is too small. In this case, consider using SMOTE (synthetic minority oversampling technique), which is discussed later in this chapter, in order to generate synthetic data.

PANDAS, CSV FILES, AND MISSING DATA

This section contains several subsections with `Python`-based code samples that create `Pandas` data frames and then replace missing values in the data frames. First we'll look at small CSV files with one column and then we'll look at small CSV files with two columns. Later we'll look at skewed CSV files as well as multi-row CSV files.

Single Column CSV Files

Listing 3.1 displays the contents of the CSV file `one_char_column1.csv` and Listing 3.2 displays the contents of `one_char_column1.py` that fills in missing values in the CSV file.

Listing 3.1: one_char_column1.csv

```
gender
Male
Male
NaN
Female
Male
```

Listing 3.2: one_char_column1.py

```python
import pandas as pd

df1 = pd.read_csv('one_char_column1.csv')

print("=> initial dataframe contents:")
print(df1)
print()

df = df1.fillna("FEMALE")
print("dataframe after fillna():")
print(df)
print()
```

Listing 3.2 starts with two `import` statements and then initializes the `Pandas` data frame `df1` with the contents of `one_char_column1.csv`, after which its contents are displayed. The next code block invokes the `fillna()` method to replace missing values with the string FEMALE. Launch the code in Listing 3.2 and you will see the following output:

```
=> initial dataframe contents:
   gender
0    Male
1    Male
2     NaN
3  Female
4    Male

dataframe after fillna():
   gender
0    Male
1    Male
2  FEMALE
3  Female
4    Male
```

Listing 3.3 displays the contents of the CSV file one_char_column2.csv and Listing 3.4 displays the contents of one_char_column2.py that fills in missing values in the CSV file.

Listing 3.3: *one_char_column2.csv*

```
gender
Male
Male
Null
Female
Male
```

Listing 3.4: *one_char_column2.py*

```
import pandas as pd

df1 = pd.read_csv('one_char_column1.csv')
```

```
print("=> initial dataframe contents:")
print(df1)
print()

df = df1.fillna("FEMALE")
print("dataframe after fillna():")
print(df)
print()
```

Listing 3.4 starts with two `import` statements and then initializes the `Pandas` data frame `df1` with the contents of `one_char_column1.csv`, after which its contents are displayed. The next code block invokes the `fillna()` method to replace missing values with the string `FEMALE`. Launch the code in Listing 3.4 and you will see the following output:

```
=> initial dataframe contents:
    gender
0     Male
1     Male
2     Null
3   Female
4     Male

df after fillna():
    gender
0     Male
1     Male
2     Null
3   Female
4     Male

gender mode: Male

=> first mapped dataframe:
    gender
0     Male
1     Male
```

```
2    Female
3       NaN
4      Male

=> second mapped dataframe:
   gender
0     Male
1     Male
2   Female
3   Female
4     Male
```

Listing 3.5 displays the contents of the CSV file one_numeric_column. csv and Listing 3.6 displays the contents of one_numeric_column.py that fills in missing values in the CSV file.

Listing 3.5: one_numeric_column.csv

```
age
19
np.nan
16
NaN
17
```

Listing 3.6: one_numeric_column.py

```python
import pandas as pd
import numpy  as np

df1 = pd.read_csv('one_numeric_column.csv')
df2 = df1.copy()
print("=> initial dataframe contents:")
print(df1)
print()

maxval = 12345
df1['age'] = df1['age'].map({'np.nan' : maxval})
```

```
print("=> dataframe after map():")
print(df1)
print()

# refresh contents of df1:
df1 = df2
df1['age'] = df1['age'].fillna(maxval)
print("=> refreshed dataframe after fillna():")
print(df1)
print()

df1 = df1.fillna(777)
print("dataframe after second fillna():")
print(df1)
print()

#print(df1.describe())
# error due to np.nan value:
#df1['age'].astype(int)

cols = df1.select_dtypes(np.number).columns
df1[cols] = df1[cols].fillna(9876)
print("df1 after third fillna():")
print(df1)
print()

# => this code block works:
#df1 = df1.replace('np.nan', 9876)
df1 = df1.replace({'np.nan': 9876})
print("df1 after replace():")
print(df1)
print()
```

Listing 3.6 starts with two `import` statements and then initializes the Pandas data frame `df1` with the contents of `one_numeric_column.csv`, after which its contents are displayed. The next code block invokes the `fillna()` method to replace missing values with the value `9876`. Launch the code in Listing 3.6 and you will see the following output:

```
=> initial dataframe contents:
        age
0        19
1   np.nan
2        16
3       NaN
4        17

=> dataframe after map():
        age
0       NaN
1   12345.0
2       NaN
3       NaN
4       NaN

=> refreshed dataframe after fillna():
        age
0        19
1   np.nan
2        16
3     12345
4        17

dataframe after second fillna():
        age
0        19
1   np.nan
2        16
3     12345
4        17
```

```
df1 after third fillna():
        age
0        19
1   np.nan
2        16
3     12345
4        17


df1 after replace():
        age
0        19
1      9876
2        16
3     12345
4        17
```

Two Column CSV Files

Listing 3.7 displays the contents of the CSV file two_columns.csv and Listing 3.8 displays the contents of two_columns.py that fills in missing values in the CSV file.

Listing 3.7: two_columns.csv

```
gender,age
Male,19
Male,np.nan
NaN,16
Female,NaN
Male,17
```

Listing 3.8: two_columns.py

```
import pandas as pd

df1 = pd.read_csv('two_columns.csv')
```

```
print("=> initial dataframe contents:")
print(df1)
print()

df1 = df1.fillna("MISSING")
print("dataframe after fillna():")
print(df1)
print()

df1 = df1.replace({'np.nan': 99})
print("dataframe after replace():")
print(df1)
print()
```

Listing 3.8 starts with two `import` statements and then initializes the Pandas data frame `df1` with the contents of `two_columns.csv`, after which its contents are displayed. The next code block invokes the `fillna()` method to replace NA values with the string MISSING, followed by a code block that replaces NaN values with 99. Launch the code in Listing 3.8 and you will see the following output:

```
=> initial dataframe contents:
   gender      age
0    Male       19
1    Male   np.nan
2     NaN       16
3  Female      NaN
4    Male       17

dataframe after fillna():
    gender      age
0     Male       19
1     Male   np.nan
2  MISSING       16
3   Female  MISSING
4     Male       17
```

```
dataframe after replace():
     gender        age
0      Male         19
1      Male         99
2   MISSING         16
3    Female    MISSING
4      Male         17
```

Listing 3.9 displays the contents of the CSV file two_columns2.csv and Listing 3.10 displays the contents of two_columns2.py that fills in missing values in the CSV file.

Listing 3.9: two_columns2.csv

```
gender,age
Male,19
Male,NaN
NaN,16
Female,18
Male,17
```

Listing 3.10: two_columns2.py

```
import pandas as pd

df1 = pd.read_csv('two_columns2.csv')
df2 = df1.copy()

print("=> initial dataframe contents:")
print(df1)
print()

# calculates the mean value on the
# 'age' column and skips NaN values:
full_avg = df1.mean()
print("full_avg:")
print(full_avg)
print()
```

```
avg = df1['age'].mean()
print("average age:",avg)
print()

# fillna() replaces NaN with avg:
df1['age'] = df1['age'].fillna(avg)
print("updated age NaN with avg:")
print(df1)
print()

# refresh contents of df1:
df1 = df2

#this does not replace NaN with avg:
#df1 = df1.replace({'NaN': avg})

mode = df1['gender'].mode()[0]
print("mode:",mode)

df1['gender'] = df1['gender'].fillna(mode)
print("updated gender NaN with mode:")
print(df1)
print()
```

Listing 3.10 starts with two `import` statements and then initializes the `Pandas` data frame `df1` with the contents of `two_columns2.csv`, after which its contents are displayed. The next code block initializes the variable `avg` with the mean value of the `age` column. This value is used to update *all* missing values in the data frame, as shown in this code block:

```
# fillna() replaces NaN with avg:
df1['age'] = df1['age'].fillna(avg)
```

The next portion of Listing 3.10 resets the contents of `df1` to its initial contents, followed by a code snippet that updates only the missing values in the `avg` column with the average, as shown here:

```
df1['age'] = df1['age'].fillna(avg)
```

The next section of code initializes the variable `mode` with the mode of the gender column and then replaces the missing values in the `gender` column with the value of the variable `mode` and then prints the updated contents of the data frame `df1`. Launch the code in Listing 3.10 and you will see the following output:

```
=> initial dataframe contents:
    gender    age
0     Male   19.0
1     Male    NaN
2      NaN   16.0
3   Female   18.0
4     Male   17.0

full_avg:
age     17.5
dtype: float64

average age: 17.5

updated all with same avg:
    gender    age
0     Male   17.5
1     Male   17.5
2      NaN   17.5
3   Female   17.5
4     Male   17.5

updated age NaN with avg:
    gender    age
0     Male   19.0
1     Male   17.5
2      NaN   16.0
3   Female   18.0
4     Male   17.0
```

```
mode: Male
updated gender NaN with mode:
    gender   age
0     Male  19.0
1     Male  17.5
2     Male  16.0
3   Female  18.0
4     Male  17.0
```

MISSING DATA AND IMPUTATION

In general, data cleaning involves or more of the following tasks, which are specific to each dataset:

- count missing data values
- remove/drop redundant columns
- assign values to missing data
- remove duplicate values
- check for incorrect values
- ensure uniformity of data
- use the Imputer class to fill with mean, median, most_frequent
- assign previous/next value to missing values
- random value imputation
- multiple imputation
- matching and hot deck-imputation

The following subsections briefly discuss some of the topics in the preceding list, along with some Python-based code samples.

Counting Missing Data Values

Listing 3.11 displays the contents of missing_values2.py that illustrates how to find the number of missing data values in a Pandas data frame.

Listing 3.11: missing_values2.py

```
import pandas as pd
import numpy as np
```

```
"""
Count NaN values in one column:
df['column name'].isna().sum()

Count NaN values in an entire data frame:
df.isna().sum().sum()

Count NaN values in one row:
df.loc[[index value]].isna().sum().sum()
"""

data = {'column1': [100,250,300,450,500,np.
nan,650,700,np.nan],
        'column2': ['X','Y',np.nan,np.
nan,'Z','A','B',np.nan,np.nan],
        'column3':['XX',np.nan,'YY','ZZ',np.nan,np.
nan,'AA',np.nan,np.nan]
        }

df = pd.DataFrame(data,columns=['column1','column2','c
olumn3'])
print("dataframe:")
print(df)

print("Missing values in 'column1':")
print(df['column1'].isna().sum())

print("Total number of missing values:")
print(df.isna().sum().sum())

print("Number of missing values for row index 7 (= row
#8):")
print(df.loc[[7]].isna().sum().sum())
```

Listing 3.11 starts with two `import` statements and a comment block that explains the purpose of several `Pandas` methods pertaining sums of values and the `isna()` method for finding NaN values in a dataset.

The next portion of Listing 3.11 initializes a dictionary with three arrays of values that are used to initialize the `Pandas` data frame `df`. Next, the missing values in `column1` are displayed, followed by the number of missing values in every column of `df`. The final code block displays the number of missing values for the row whose index is 7. Launch the code in Listing 3.11 and you will see the following output:

```
dataframe:
   column1 column2 column3
0    100.0       X      XX
1    250.0       Y     NaN
2    300.0     NaN      YY
3    450.0     NaN      ZZ
4    500.0       Z     NaN
5      NaN       A     NaN
6    650.0       B      AA
7    700.0     NaN     NaN
8      NaN     NaN     NaN
Missing values in 'column1':
2
Total number of missing values:
11
Number of missing values for row index 7 (= row #8):
2
```

Next, navigate to this link where you will find additional `Python` code samples for data cleaning:

https://lvngd.com/blog/data-cleaning-with-python-pandas/

Drop Redundant Columns

Listing 3.12 displays the contents of `drop_columns.py` that illustrates how to remove redundant columns from a `Pandas` data frame.

Listing 3.12: drop_columns.py

```
import pandas as pd
```

```
# specify a valid CSV file here:
df1 = pd.read_csv("my_csv_file.csv") # <= specify your
own CSV file


# remove redundant columns:
df2 = df1.drop(['url'],axis=1)


# remove columns with over 50% missing values
df3 = df2.dropna(thresh=half_count,axis=1)
```

Listing 3.12 initializes the `Pandas` data frame `df1` with the contents of the CSV file `my_csv_file.csv` and then initializes the `Pandas` data frame `df2` with the contents of `df1`, and then drops the column `url`, or some other column that exists in your CSV file. Finally, the `Pandas` data frame `df3` is initialized with the contents of `Pandas` data frame `df2`, after which columns are dropped if they have more than 50% missing values.

Remove Duplicate Rows

Data deduplication refers to the task of removing row-level duplicate data values. Listing 3.13 displays the contents of `duplicates.csv` and Listing 3.14 displays the content of `duplicates.sh` that removes the duplicate rows and creates the CSV file `no_duplicates.csv` that contains unique rows.

Listing 3.13: duplicates.csv

```
Male,19,190,0
Male,19,190,0
Male,15,180,0
Male,15,180,0
Female,16,150,0
Female,16,150,0
Female,17,170,0
Female,17,170,0
Male,19,160,0
Male,19,160,0
```

Listing 3.14: remove-duplicates.sh

```
filename1="duplicates.csv"
filename2="no_duplicates.csv"


cat $filename1 | sort |uniq > $filename2
```

Listing 3.14 is straightforward: after initializing the variables `filename1` and `filename2` with the names of the input and output files, respectively, the only remaining code snippet contains Unix pipe ("|") with a sequence of commands. The left-most command displays the contents of the input file, which is redirected to the `sort` command that sorts the input rows. The result of the sort command is redirected to the `uniq` command, which removes duplicate rows, and this result set is redirected to the file specified in the variable `filename2`.

Keep in mind that the `sort` followed by `uniq` command is required: this is how the `uniq` command can remove adjacent duplicate rows. Launch the code in Listing 3.14 and you will see the output that is displayed in Listing 3.15.

Listing 3.15: no_duplicates.csv

```
Male,19,190,0
Female,16,150,0
Female,17,170,0
Male,15,180,0
Male,19,160,0
Male,19,190,0
```

Display Duplicate Rows

The preceding example shows you how to find the unique rows and the code sample in Listing 3.16 in this section shows you how to find the duplicate rows.

Listing 3.16: find-duplicates.sh

```
filename1="duplicates.csv"
sorted="sorted.csv"
unique="unique.csv"
multiple="multiple.csv"
```

```
# sorted rows:
cat $filename1 | sort > $sorted

# unique rows:
cat $sorted | uniq > $unique

# duplicates rows:
diff -u $sorted $unique |sed -e '1,3d' -e 's/^ //' -e
's/-//' > $multiple
```

Listing 3.16 starts by initializing the variables `filename1`, `sorted`, `unique`, and `multiple` to names of CSV files, where only filename1 is a non-empty file.

The next portion of Listing 3.16 consists of three lines of code that create three text files:

```
sorted.csv
unique.csv
multiple.csv
```

The file `sorted.csv` contains the sorted set of rows from `duplicates.csv`, and the file `unique.csv` contains the unique rows in `sorted.csv`. Therefore, the duplicate rows are the rows that appear in `sorted.csv` that do not appear in `unique.csv`. Launch the code in Listing 3.16 and then inspect the contents of `multiple.csv`.

The third line with the `diff` command generates the list of lines in $sorted that are not in $uniq, which are of course the duplicate lines. In addition, the output of the `diff` command is redirected to the `sed` command that does three things:

- Remove the first three text lines.
- Remove an initial space character.
- Remove an initial "-" character.

After the `sed` command has completed, the output is redirected to the file $multiple that contains the duplicate rows.

Uniformity of Data Values

An example of uniformity of data involves verifying that the data in a given feature contains the same units measure. For example, the following set of values have numeric values that are in a narrow range but the units of measure are incorrect:

```
50mph
50kph
100mph
20kph
```

Listing 3.19 displays the contents of same_units.sh that illustrates how to ensure that a set of strings have the same unit of measure.

Listing 3.19: same_units.sh

```
strings="120kph 100mph 50kph"
new_unit="fps"

for x in `echo $strings`
do
  number=`echo $x | tr -d [a-z][A-Z]`
  unit=`echo $x | tr -d [0-9]`
  echo "initial: $x"
  new_num="${number}${new_unit}"
  echo "new_num: $new_num"
  echo
done
```

Listing 3.19 starts by initializing the variables strings and new_unit, followed by a for loop that iterates through each string in the strings variable. During each iteration, the variables number and unit are initialized with the characters and digits, respectively, in the current string represented by the loop variable x.

Next, the variable new_num is initialized as the concatenation of the contents of number and new_unit. Launch the code in Listing 3.19 and you will see the following output:

```
initial: 120kph
new_num: 120fps
initial: 100mph
new_num: 100fps
```

```
initial: 50kph
new_num: 50fps
```

Too Many Missing Data Values

Datasets with mostly `N/A` values, which is to say, 80% or more are `N/A` or `NaN` values, is always daunting, but not necessarily hopeless. As a simple first step, you can drop rows that contain `N/A` values, which might result in a loss of 99% of the data. A variation of the preceding all-or-nothing step for handling datasets with a majority of `N/A` values is as follows:

- Use a kNN imputer to fill missing values in high value columns.
- Drop low-priority columns that have > 50% missing values.
- Use a KNN imputer (again) to fill the remaining missing values.
- Try using 3 or 5 as the # of nearest neighbors.

The preceding sequence attempts to prune insignificant data in order to concentrate on reconstructing the higher priority columns through data imputation. Of course, there is no guaranteed methodology for salvaging such a dataset, so you need some ingenuity as you experiment with data sets containing highly limited data values. If the dataset is highly imbalanced, consider *oversampling* before you drop columns and/or rows, which is discussed in Chapter 2.

Categorical Data

Categorical values are discrete and can easily be encoded by specifying a number for each category. If a category has n distinct values, then visualize the `nxn` identity matrix: each row represents one of the distinct values.

This technique is called "one hot encoding,", and you can use the `One-HotEncoder` class in `scikit-learn` by specifying the dataset `X` and also the column index to perform one hot encoding:

```
from scikit-learn.preprocessing import OneHotEncoder
ohc = OneHotEncoder(categorical_features = [0])
X = onehotencoder.fit_transform(X).toarray()
```

Since each one hot encoded row contains one 1 and (n-1) zero values, this technique is inefficient with n is large. Another technique involves the `Pandas map()` function that replaces string values with a single column that contains numeric values. For example, the following code block replaces `Male` and `Female` with 0 and 1, respectively:

```
values = {'Male' : 0, 'Female' : 1}
df['gender'] = df['gender'].map(values)
```

A variation of the preceding is the following code block:

```
data['gender'].replace(0, 'Female',inplace=True)
data['gender'].replace(1, 'Male',inplace=True)
```

Another variation of the preceding code is this code block:

```
data['gender'].replace([0,1],['Male','Female'],inplace
=True)
```

Keep in mind that the Pandas map() function converts invalid entries to NaN.

Data Inconsistency

Data inconsistency occurs when distinct values are supposed to be the same value, such as "smith" and "SMITH" instead of "Smith." Another example would be "YES," "Yes," "YS," and "ys" instead of "yes." In all cases except for "ys," you can convert all the other strings to lowercase, which replaces all the strings with smith or yes, respectively.

Alternatively, the Python-based Fuzzy Wuzzy library can be helpful if there are too many distinct values to specify manually. This module identifies strings that are likely to be the same by comparing two strings and generating a numeric value, such that values closer to each other are more likely to represent the same string.

Mean Value Imputation

Listing 3.20 displays the contents of mean_imputation.py that shows you how to replace missing values with the mean value of each feature.

Listing 3.20: mean_imputation.py

```
import numpy as np
import pandas as pd
import random

filename="titanic.csv"
df = pd.read_csv(filename)
```

```
# display null values:
print("=> Initial df.isnull().sum():")
print(df.isnull().sum())
print()


# replace missing ages with mean value:
df['age'] = df['age'].fillna(df['age'].mean())


"""
Or use median(), min(), or max():
df['age'] = df['age'].fillna(df['age'].median())
df['age'] = df['age'].fillna(df['age'].min())
df['age'] = df['age'].fillna(df['age'].max())
"""


# FILL MISSING DECK VALUES WITH THE mode():
mode = df['deck'].mode()[0]
#df['deck'] = df['deck'].fillna(mode)

print("=> new age and deck values:")
print([df[['deck','age']]])
```

Listing 3.20 starts with several `import` statements, followed by initializing the variable `df` with the contents of the specified CSV file. The next code snippet calculates the number of rows with missing values on a column-by-column basis. The next code snippet replaces the missing values with the mean value of the available values, also on a column-by-column basis. In addition, a commented code shows you how invoke the `median()`, `min()`, and `max()` values, respectively, that you can specify instead of the `mean()` if you wish to do so.

The next code snippet initializes the variable mode with the mode value of the deck feature, followed by a `print()` statement that displays the values for the `deck` and `age` features. Launch the code in Listing 3.20 and you will see the following output:

```
=> Initial df.isnull().sum():
survived          0
pclass            0
```

```
sex                   0
age                 177
sibsp                 0
parch                 0
fare                  0
embarked              2
class                 0
who                   0
adult_male            0
deck                688
embark_town           2
alive                 0
alone                 0
dtype: int64

=> new age and deck values:
[      deck          age
0        C   22.000000
1        C   38.000000
2        C   26.000000
3        C   35.000000
4        C   35.000000
..      ...         ...
886      C   27.000000
887      B   19.000000
888      C   29.699118
889      C   26.000000
890      C   32.000000

[891 rows x 2 columns]]
```

Is a Zero Value Valid or Invalid?

In general, replacing a missing numeric value with zero is a risky choice: this value is obviously incorrect if the values of a feature are positive numbers between 1,000 and 5,000 (or some other range of positive numbers). For a feature that has numeric values, replacing a missing value with the mean of existing values can be better than the value zero (unless the average equals zero); also consider using the median value. For categorical data, consider using the mode to replace a missing value.

There are situations in which you can use the mean of existing values to impute missing values but not the value zero, and vice versa. As a first example, suppose that an attribute contains the height in centimeters of a set of persons. In this case, the mean could be a reasonable imputation, whereas 0 suffers from:

1. It's an invalid value (nobody has height 0).

2. It will skew statistical quantities such as the mean and variance.

You might be tempted to use the mean instead of 0 when the minimum allowable value is a positive number, but use caution when working with highly imbalanced datasets. As a second example, consider a small community of 50 residents with:

1. Forty-five 45 people have an average annual income of 50,000 US$.

2. Four other residents have an annual income of 10,000,000 US$.

3. One resident has an unknown annual income.

Although the preceding example might seem contrived, it's likely that the median income is preferable to the mean income, and certainly better than imputing a value of 0.

As a third example, suppose that a company generates weekly sales reports for multiple office branches, and a new office has been opened but has yet to make any sales. In this case, the use of the mean to impute missing values for this branch would produce fictitious results. Hence, it makes sense to use the value 0 for all sales-related quantities, which will accurately reflect the sales-related status of the new branch.

DATA NORMALIZATION

Normalization is the process of scaling numeric columns in a dataset so that they have a common scale. In addition, the scaling is performed as follows:

1. scaling values to the range [0,1]

2. without losing information

3. without distorting any differences that exist in the ranges of values

You can perform data normalization via the function `MinMaxScaler()` in the `Scikit-Learn` library.

Assigning Classes to Data

Listing 3.30 displays the contents of `product_prices.csv` and Listing 3.31 displays the contents of `assign_classes.py` that illustrates how to assign a class value to each row in a dataset.

Listing 3.30: product_prices.csv

```
item,price
product1,100
product2,200
product3,250
product4,300
product5,400
```

Listing 3.31: assign_classes.py

```python
import pandas as pd

df = pd.read_csv("product_prices.csv")
print("contents of df:")
print(df)
print()

# define class ranges:
def class_value2(y):
  if y<=100:
    return '(1) 0 - 100'
  elif y<=200:
    return '(2) 100 - 200'
  elif y<=250:
    return '(3) 200 - 250'
  else:
    return '(4) 250+'
```

```
def class_value(y):
  if y<=100:
    return '1'
  elif y<=200:
    return '2'
  elif y<=250:
    return '3'
  else:
    return '4'

df['class1'] = df['price'].apply(class_value)
df['class2'] = df['price'].apply(class_value2)

print("contents of df:")
print(df)
```

Listing 3.31 initializes the Pandas data frame df with the contents of the CSV file product_prices.csv (displayed in Listing 3.30) and displays its contents. The next portion of Listing 3.31 is the Python function class_value2 that returns a string whose contents are a range of values that are based on the parameter y. For example, if y at most 100, the function returns the string (1) 0 - 100, and similar strings for larger values of y.

The next portion of Listing 3.31 is the Python function class_value that returns a string 1, 2, 3, or 4, depending on the parameter y. The last portion of Listing 3.31 initializes the column class1 and class2 in df, respectively, by invoking the apply() method with the Python functions class_value and class_value2. Launch the code in Listing 3.31 and you will see the following output:

```
contents of df:
       item  price
0  product1    100
1  product2    200
2  product3    250
3  product4    300
4  product5    400
```

```
contents of df:
        item  price class1          class2
0   product1    100      1    (1)  0 - 100
1   product2    200      2    (2) 100 - 200
2   product3    250      3    (3) 200 - 250
3   product4    300      4         (4) 250+
4   product5    400      4         (4) 250+
```

Other Data Cleaning Tasks

As a quick review, here is a list of additional tasks that belong to data cleaning that might be relevant to a given dataset:

- detect outliers/anomalies
- resolve missing data
- resolve incorrect data
- resolve duplicate data
- remove hidden control characters (ex: \t, ^L, ^M)
- remove HTML tags (ex: <div>, <a>, and so forth)
- handle diacritical marks
- check for gaps in sequences of data
- check for unusual distributions
- examine the actual data instead of relying on documentation

HANDLING CATEGORICAL DATA

A feature containing categorical data can suffer from various issues, such as missing data, invalid data, or inconsistently formatted data. The following section discusses examples of inconsistent categorical data followed by a section that discusses how to map categorical data to numeric values.

Processing Inconsistent Categorical Data

This section contains examples of processing inconsistent data values. For features that have very low cardinality, consider dropping those features, and and do the same for numeric columns with zero or very low variance.

Next, check the contents of categorical columns for inconsistent spellings or errors. For example, suppose that a feature contains the values M and F (for male and female) along with a mixture of gender-related strings, some of which are in the following list:

```
male
Male
female
Female
m
f
M
F
```

The preceding categorical values for gender can be replaced with two categorical values (unless you have a valid reason to retain some of the other values). Moreover, if you are training a model whose analysis involves a single gender, then you need to determine which rows (if any) of a dataset must be excluded. Also check categorical data columns for redundant or missing whitespaces.

Check for data values that have multiple data types, such as a numerical column with numbers as numerals and some numbers as strings or objects. Also ensure consistent data formats: numbers as integer or floating numbers and ensure that dates have the same format (e.g., do not mix a mm/dd/yyyy date format with another date format, such as dd/mm/yyyy).

Mapping Categorical Data to Numeric Values

Character data is often called categorical data, examples of which include people's names, home or work addresses, email addresses, and so forth. Many types of categorical data involve short lists of values. For example, the days of the week and the months in a year involve seven and twelve distinct values, respectively. Notice that the days of the week have a relationship: each day has a previous day and a next day, and similarly for the months of a year.

On the other hand, the colors of an automobile are independent of each other: the color red is not "better" or "worse" than the color blue. However, cars of a certain color can have a statistically higher number of accidents, which is of interest to insurance companies, but we won't address this case here.

There are several well-known techniques for mapping categorical values to a set of numeric values. A simple example where you need to perform this conversion involves the gender feature in the Titanic dataset. This feature is one of the relevant features for training a machine learning model. The gender feature has {M, F} as its set of values. As you will see later in this chapter, Pandas makes it very easy to convert the pair of values {M, F} to the pair of values {0,1}.

Another mapping technique involves mapping a set of categorical values to a set of consecutive integer values. For example, the set {Red, Green, Blue} can be mapped to the set of integers {0,1,2}. The set {Male, Female} can be mapped to the set of integers {0,1}. The days of the week can be mapped to {0,1,2,3,4,5,6}. Note that the first day of the week depends on the country: in some cases it's Sunday and in other cases its Monday.

Another technique is called *one-hot encoding*, which converts each value to a *vector* (check Wikipedia if you need a refresher regarding vectors). Thus, {Male, Female} can be represented by the vectors [1,0] and [0,1], and the colors {Red, Green, Blue} can be represented by the vectors [1,0,0], [0,1,0], and [0,0,1].

If you vertically "line up" the two vectors for gender, they form a 2x2 identity matrix, and doing the same for the colors {R,G,B} will form a 3x3 identity matrix, as shown here:

```
[1,0,0]
[0,1,0]
[0,0,1]
```

This technique generalizes in a straightforward manner: if you have n distinct categorical values, you can map each of those values to one of the vectors in an nxn identity matrix.

As another example, the set of titles {"Intern","Junior", "Mid-Range","Senior", "Project Leader","Dev Manager"} have a hierarchical relationship in terms of their salaries (which can also overlap, but we'll gloss over that detail for now).

Another set of categorical data involves the season of the year: {"Spring", "Summer", "Autumn", "Winter"} and while these values are generally independent of each other, there are cases in which the season is significant. For example, the values for the monthly rainfall, average temperature, crime rate, and foreclosure rate can depend on the season, month, week, or even the day of the year.

If a feature has a large number of categorical values, then a one-hot encoding will produce many additional columns for each data point. Since the majority of the values in the new columns equal 0, this can increase the sparsity of the dataset, which in turn can result in more overfitting and hence adversely affect the accuracy of machine learning algorithms that you adopt during the training process.

Another solution is to use a sequence-based solution in which N categories are mapped to the integers 1, 2, . . ., N. Another solution involves examining the row frequency of each categorical value. For example, suppose that N equals 20, and there are 3 categorical values for 95% of the values for a given feature. You can try the following:

1. Assign the values 1, 2, and 3 to those three categorical values.

2. Assign numeric values that reflect the relative frequency of those categorical values.

3. Assign the category "OTHER" to the remaining categorical values.

4. Delete the rows whose categorical values belong to the 5%.

DATA WRANGLING

Data wrangling means different things to different people, which might cause some confusion unless people clarify what they mean when they talk about data wrangling. Data wrangling involves multiple steps that can include transforming one or more files. Here are some of the interpretations of data wrangling:

- It's part of a sequence of steps.
- Data wrangling transforms datasets.
- Data wrangling is essentially the same as data cleaning.

This book adopts the approach of the first and second bullet items but not of the third. Navigate to the following link that lists data wrangling as part of a six-step process:

https://en.wikipedia.org/wiki/Data_wrangling

In addition to the steps outlined in the preceding link, data wrangling can also involve the following task:

- transforming datasets from one format into another format (convert)
- creating new data sets from subsets of columns in existing data sets (extract)

As you can see, the preceding steps differentiate between converting data to a different format versus extracting data from multiple datasets to create new datasets. The conversion process can be considered a data cleaning task if only the first step is performed; that is, there is no extraction step.

One additional comment: the interpretation of data wrangling in this chapter is convenient but it's not a universally accepted standard definition. Hence, you are free to adopt your own interpretation of data wrangling (versus data cleaning) if you find one that better suits your needs.

Data Transformation: What Does This Mean?

In general, data cleaning involves a single data source (not necessarily in a CSV format), with some type of modification to the content of the data source (e.g., filling missing values, changing date formats, and so forth), without creating a second data source.

For example, suppose that the data source is a MySQL table called employees that contains employee-related information. After data cleaning tasks on the employees table are completed, the result will still be named the employees table. In database terminology, data cleaning is somewhat analogous to executing a SQL statement that involves a SELECT on a single table.

On the other hand, if two CSV files contain different date formats and you need to create a single CSV file that is based on the date columns, then there will be some type of conversion process that could be one of the following:- Convert the first date format to the second date format, or

- Convert the second date format to the first date format, or
- Convert both date formats to a third date format

In the case of financial data, you are likely to also encounter different currencies, which involves a conversion rate between a pair of currencies. Since currency conversion rates fluctuate, you need to decide the exchange rate to use for the data, which can be:

- the exchange rate during the date that the CSV files were generated
- the current currency exchange rate
- some other mechanism

In addition, you might also need to convert the CSV files to XML documents, where the latter might be required to conform to an XML Schema, and perhaps also conform to XBRL, which is a requirement for business reporting purposes:

https://en.wikipedia.org/wiki/XBRL

As mentioned previously, data transformation can involve two or more data sources in order to create yet another data source whose attributes are in the required format. Here are four scenarios of data transformation with just two data sources A and B, where data from A and from B are combined in order to create data source C, where A, B, and C can have different file formats:

- all attributes in A and all attributes in B
- all attributes in A and some attributes in B
- a subset of the attributes in A and all attributes in B
- a subset of the attributes in A and some attributes in B

In database terminology, data transformation is somewhat analogous to executing a SQL statement that involves a SELECT on two or more database tables with a JOIN clause. Such SQL statements typically involve a subset of columns from each database table, which would correspond to selecting a subset of the features in the data sources.

Keep in mind there is also the scenario involving the *concatenation* of two or more data sources. If all data sources have the same attributes, then their concatenation is straightforward, but you might also need to check for duplicate values. For example, if you want to load multiple CSV files into a database table that does not allow duplicates, then one solution involves concatenating the CSV files from the command line and then excluding the duplicate rows.

SUMMARY

This chapter started with several Pandas code samples that use Pandas to read CSV files and then calculate statistical values such as the mean, median, mode, and standard deviation of the data values.

Then you learned how to use Pandas to handle missing values in CSV files, starting with CSV files that contain a single column, followed by two-column CSV files. In addition, you saw how to work with multicolumn CSV files, such as the Titanic titanic.csv CSV file.

## CHAPTER 4

INTRODUCTION TO STATISTICS

This chapter discusses concepts in statistics. As such, you will learn about rudimentary aspects of statistics, how to detect normally distributed datasets, various types of probability distributions, and useful metrics associated with a confusion matrix.

Something to keep in mind is that currently there are more than 100 statistical tests available on Wikipedia:

https://en.wikipedia.org/wiki/Category:Statistical_tests

Fortunately, it's not necessary to learn about all those tests. This book discusses a modest subset of the tests that are available in the preceding link, which is where you can learn about other tests interest you.

The first section of this chapter briefly describes the need for statistics, followed by some well-known terminology in statistics. This section also introduces the content of random variable, as well as the difference between discrete and continuous random variables.

The second section introduces basic statistical concepts, such as *mean*, *median*, *mode*, *variance*, and *standard deviation*, along with Python examples that show you how to calculate these quantities. You will also learn about Chebyshev's inequality, dispersion, and sampling techniques.

The third section shows you tests that you can perform in order to detect normally distributed data, such as D'Agostino's test, Pearson's correlation coefficient, and augmented Dickey-Fuller. In addition, you will learn about the acronyms PDF, CDF, and PMF.

The fourth section introduces continuous probability distributions, such as chi-square, Gaussian, and uniform distribution. You will also learn about discrete probability distributions, such as Bernoulli, binomial, exponential, and Poisson distribution. The section also has information about non-Gaussian distributions and some of the causes of such distributions.

The fifth section discusses metrics for linear regression, including MAE, MSE, RMSE, and MMR. Then you will learn about skewness and kurtosis, and other concepts such as the CLT, causality and the contrapositive, and statistical inferences.

The sixth section introduces the well-known confusion matrix that is very useful for machine learning classification algorithms, along with type I errors, type II errors, and the metrics accuracy, precision, and recall. This section also discusses the ROC curve and the AUC curve. In addition, you will learn about the F1 score and related scores, such as F2, and F3 that are useful for classification algorithms.

BASIC CONCEPTS IN STATISTICS

Statistics are useful for describing the characteristics of a dataset, which can be a sample of a population. A *population* is a set or a collection of entities, where the latter can be people, inanimate objects, or abstractions of a physical entity. A *sample* is a subset of the population that is selected for study.

A *paired sample* is a sample for which data is collected twice from the same group or entity. An *independent sample* involves two samples whose values are from two different populations.

A *variable* is a characteristic that can have different values (more about this later). A quantitative variable has values that are real numbers, whereas a qualitative variable consists of categorical data (i.e., string values). The value of a variable is called an *observation* or *measurement*.

A *discrete variable* is a variable that is countable in the mathematical sense. Hence, a discrete variable can consist of a finite set of values as well as a set of values that can be "mapped" to the set of positive integers.

A *continuous variable* consists of an uncountably infinite set of values, such as the real number line. Note that irrational values must be approximated, which effectively means that the values of a continuous variable are treated as rational values.

Inferential Statistics Versus Descriptive Statistics

Descriptive statistics are useful when you need a summary of the nature of the data in a dataset, which includes the mean, median, standard deviation, and so forth.

Inferential statistics involves making inferences from a sample of data from the population. This technique is used in various scenarios, such as predicting voter outcomes in elections, checking trucks for food spoilage, and so forth.

This approach is more cost effective when a population is so large that it's impractical to validate every item in the population.

The following websites offer more information on the topic of statistics:

https://careerfoundry.com/en/blog/data-analytics/inferential-vs-descriptive-statistics

https://towardsdatascience.com/statistics-lecture-1-227f934924d9

Descriptive statistics consists of the collection, organization, and summarization of data. Examples include: mean, median, percentiles, counts, and so forth.

Example: Average healthcare spending per capita by state governments in 2005–2006 was $2845.

Inferential statistics consists of methods for drawing and measuring the reliability of conclusions about a population, leveraging a sample. Examples include: estimates, hypothesis tests, and relationships among variables and predictions.

Example: By the year 2035, 25% of the U.S. population will be 65 years of age or older.

Various types of descriptive statistics that you can obtain using ordinal data (discussed in Chapter 1) are listed below:

- frequency distribution
- measures of central tendency: mode and/or median
- measures of variability: range

A *frequency distribution* pertains to the distribution of data in a dataset. You can summarize the distribution via a frequency table, a histogram, or a pivot table (among others). If possible, try to display the data in a dataset in a histogram, which might provide some clues regarding the distribution of the data.

RANDOM VARIABLES

A *random variable* is a variable that can have multiple values, and where each value has an associated probability of occurrence. For example, if X is a random variable whose values are the outcomes of tossing a well-balanced die, then the values of X are the numbers in the set {1,2,3,4,5,6}. Moreover, each of those values can occur with equal probability (which is 1/6).

In the case of two well-balanced dice, let X be a random variable whose values can be any of the numbers in the set {2,3,4, . . . , 12}. The set of associated probabilities for the different values for X are listed here:

```
{1/36,2/36,3/36,4/36,5/36,6/36,5/36,4/36,3/26,2/36,1/3
6}
```

Discrete Versus Continuous Random Variables

The preceding section contains examples of *discrete* random variables because the list of possible values is either finite or countably infinite (such as the set of integers). As an aside, the set of rational numbers is also countably infinite, but the set of irrational numbers and also the set of real numbers are both uncountably infinite (proofs are available online).

The set of probabilities of a random variable must form a probability distribution, which means that the probability values are nonnegative. In the case of a discrete probability distribution, the sum of the probabilities must equal 1, whereas for a continuous probability distribution, the area under the curve (i.e., between the curve and the horizontal axis) must equal 1.

A *continuous* random variable is a random variable whose values can be *any* number in a given interval such as [a,b] (where a<b), which contains an uncountably infinite number of values. For example, the amount of time required to perform a task is represented by a continuous random variable.

Moreover, a continuous random variable has a probability distribution that is represented as a continuous function. The constraint for such a variable is that the area under the curve equals 1 (sometimes calculated via a mathematical integral).

Confounding Variables

A *confounding variable* (aka confounding factor) is a variable that influences the dependent variable and the independent variable, which creates a spurious association that in turn can lead to erroneous conclusions.

A famous example is the observation that an increase in ice cream consumption during the summer in a city coincided with an increase in crime. We would not assert that ice cream consumption leads to greater crime: temperature is an underlying confounding variable.

Interestingly, one recent study suggests that "the seemingly protective effect of vegetable intake against cardiovascular disease risk is very likely to be accounted for by bias from residual confounding factors, related to differences in socioeconomic situation and lifestyle" (Pinkstone, 2022, para. 6).

Counterfactual Analysis

RCT is an acronym for *randomized controlled trials*, where such trials establish causality between variables via counterfactual analysis. Examples of RCT include drug and vaccine testing. RCT was also instrumental in analyzing the impact of smoking as a cause of cancer.

However, the ability of RCT experiments to determine causality is only possible for a small number of variables, and the experiments themselves are also challenging to set up.

Interestingly, AirBnB developed a new technique called artificial counterfactual estimation (ACE) that reproduces counterfactual outcomes by a combination of machine learning techniques and causal inference.

An explanation of a counterfactual is here: *https://ml-retrospectives. github.io/neurips2020/camera_ready/5.pdf*

More information and a description of ACE can be found on the following two sites:

https://medium.com/airbnb-engineering/artificial-counterfactual-estimation-ace-machine-learning-based-causal-inference-at-airbnb-ee32ee4d0512
https://medium.datadriveninvestor.com/beyond-statistics-a0087622cbfc

Sampling Techniques in Statistics

There are several well-known sampling techniques (with varying degrees of complexity), some of which are listed below:

- random sampling
- systematic sampling
- stratified sampling
- cluster sampling

Random sampling (aka probability sampling) involves random samples of observations from a population, where samples have an equal probability of being selected. This method reduces the bias in the sample.

Systematic sampling involves selecting samples in a "periodic" fashion. For example, suppose that you want to form three teams from a roomful of people. Next, starting from a convenient location in the room (e.g., front left corner or rear right corner), the first three adjacent people will count off "one," "two," and "three," respectively. Counting will continue in this sequence until everyone has designated one of those three numbers.

Stratified sampling involves subdividing a population into subgroups (called "strata"), after which a random sample is selected from each subgroup. The selection process continues until the sample contains the specified number of samples.

Cluster sampling involves the following steps:

1. Subdivide a population into subgroups (aka "clusters").

2. Randomly select some of the subgroups.

3. Randomly select samples from the chosen subgroups.

Hence, cluster sampling involves randomly selecting people from each cluster instead of selecting people from the entire group. Note that if you specify only one cluster, then cluster sampling is the same as random sampling.

MULTIPLE RANDOM VARIABLES

This section briefly discusses some basic properties (without derivations) of multiple random variables. If X1 and X2 are two random variables and Y = X1+X2 then the following formulas are valid:

```
mean(Y) = mean(X1) + mean(X2)
var(Y)  = var(X1)  + var(X2) + 2*Covariance(X1,X2)
```

For the general case involving a sequence of random variables X1, X2, X3, ..., Xn, we have the following formulas:

```
Y = X1 + X2 + ... + Xn

             n
mean(Y)  = SUM mean(Xi)
            i=0
```

```
              n
var(Y)   = SUM var (Xi) + SUM Covariance(Xi,Xj)
              i=0                i<j
```

If `Xi` and `Xj` are pairwise independent, then `covariance(Xi,Xj) = 0`, and therefore we have:

```
              n
var(Y)   = SUM var (Xi)
              i=0
```

Working With Two or More Variables

There are several constructs that you can use when you need to work with two or more variables, some of which are listed below:

- contingency table (useful for two categorical variables)
- contour plot
- hexagonal binning
- violin plot

Types of Convergence for Random Variables

Consider the following sequence of random variables `X1, X2, X3, ...` that can exhibit the following types of convergence, shown in increasing order:

- convergence in mean
- convergence in probability
- convergence in distribution

"Increasing order" indicates the following: convergence in mean (the strongest) implies convergence in probability, which in turn implies convergence in distribution (the weakest).

Using informal terminology, a sequence `{X1, X2, ..., Xn}` "convergences in mean" to `X` indicates that the difference `|X - Xn|` becomes arbitrarily small as `n` becomes arbitrarily large. Similar comments apply to convergence in probability and distribution.

BASIC CONCEPTS IN STATISTICS

This section discusses the mean, median, and mode, followed by a section that discusses variance and standard deviation. Feel free to skim (or skip) this section if you are already familiar with these concepts. Here is a summary of different types of measures in statistics:

- Measures of central tendency: the mean, median, mode, and midrange.
- Measures of variation: the range, variance, and standard deviation.
- Percentiles, deciles, and quartiles: find the relative location of a data point in a dataset.

For the following subsections, let's suppose that the set $X = \{x1, \ldots, xn\}$ is a set of numbers that can be positive, negative, integer-valued, or decimal values.

The Mean

The *mean* of the numbers in the set X is the average of the values. For example, if the set X consists of $\{-10, 35, 75, 100\}$, then the mean equals $(-10 + 35 + 75 + 100)/4 = 50$. If the set X consists of $\{2, 2, 2, 2\}$, then the mean equals $(2+2+2+2)/4 = 2$. As you can see, the mean value is not necessarily one of the values in the set.

Keep in mind that the mean is sensitive to outliers. For example, the mean of the set of numbers $\{1,2,3,4\}$ is 2.5, whereas the mean of the set of number $\{1,2,3,4,1000\}$ is 202. Since the formulas for the variance and standard deviation involve the mean of a set of numbers, both of these terms are also more sensitive to outliers. The mean is suitable for symmetric distributions without outliers.

The Weighted Mean

The weighted mean calculates a sum of a set of values where some (possibly all) values in the set are multiplied by different weights. The weighted sum is calculated in the same manner as the expected value. For example, suppose that we have the sets V and W as shown here:

```
V = {1, 2, 3, 4}
W = {0.5, 2, 1.5, -2}
```

Then the weighted average WA is calculated as follows:

```
         4
WA = SUM (vi * wi)/4
       i=1
```

Hence, the weighted sum WA equals the following value:

```
WA = [1*0.5 + 2*2 + 3*1.5 +4*(-2)]/4 = (0.5+4+4.5-8)/4
   = 1/4
```

The Median

The *median* of the numbers (sorted in increasing or decreasing order) in the set X is the middle value in the set of values, which means that half the numbers in the set are less than the median and half the numbers in the set are greater than the median. Note that the median is not necessarily one of the values in the given set.

For example, if the set X consists of {35,75,100}, then the *median* equals 75 because this value partitions the set X into two sets having the same cardinality. On the other hand, if the set X consists of {-10,35,75,100}, then the *median* equals 55 because 55 is the average of the two numbers 35 and 75. As you can see, half the numbers are less than 55 and half the numbers are greater than 55. If the set X consists of {2,2,2,2}, then the *median* equals 2.

By contrast, the median is much less sensitive to outliers than the mean. For example, the median of the set of numbers {1,2,3,4} is 2.5, and the median of the set of numbers {1,2,3,4,1000} is 3.

As you can see from the preceding simple example, the median works better than the mean for skewed distributions or data with outliers.

The Mean Versus the Median

The preceding section stated that the median works better than the mean for skewed distributions or data with outliers, which is true for many situations. However, there are cases in which the mean is preferred instead of the median, even with a skewed dataset. Specifically, we prefer the median when we want to *avoid* an outlier, whereas we prefer the mean when we *want* the outlier.

More information on the mean and median can be found here: *https:// towardsdatascience.com/mean-or-median-choose-based-on-the-decision-not-the-distribution-f951215c1376*

For example, suppose that the values in set A consists of {$2,$4,$5,$6,$8}, so the mean and median are both $5. In addition, suppose that the set B contains the values {$2,$3,$4,$6,$1000000}, so the mean is $200,003 and median is $4. Hence, it's reasonable to use the mean for set A and the median for set B: this is a logical choice, because 1000000 in set B appears to be an outlier with respect to the other values in set B.

Now let's assume that the values in A and B represent monetary rewards, where all outcomes in A and in B have equal probability (i.e., 1/5). Then the potential payoff for set A is much smaller than the potential payoff for set B. In the former case, the maximum you can receive is $8, whereas in the latter case, you might receive $1000000.

As you can see, set A is close to symmetric with median equal to 5, whereas set B is highly asymmetric whose median is smaller than the mean. In essence, we *prefer* set B because it contains an outlier that can lead to a positive outcome.

The Mode

The *mode* of the numbers (sorted in increasing or decreasing order) in the set X is the most frequently occurring value, which means that there can be more than one such value. The median is frequently the preferred statistic for skewed distributions or distributions with outliers.

As a simple example, if the set X consists of {2,2,2,2}, then the *mode* equals 2. However, if X is the set of numbers {2,4,5,5,6,8}, then the number 5 occurs twice and the other numbers occur only once, so the *mode* equals 5.

If X is the set of numbers {2,2,4,5,5,6,8}, then the numbers 2 and 5 occur twice and the other numbers occur only once, so the *mode* equals 2 and 5. A set that has two modes is called *bimodal*, and a set that has more than two modes is called *multimodal*.

One other scenario involves sets that have numbers with the same frequency and they are all different. In this case, the mode does not provide meaningful information, and one alternative is to partition the numbers into subsets and then select the largest subset. For example, if set X has the values {1,2,15,16,17,25,35,50}, we can partition the set into subsets whose elements are in range that are multiples of ten, which results in the subsets {1,2}, {15,16,17}, {25}, {35}, and {50}. The largest subset is {15,16,17}, so we could select the number 16 as the mode.

As another example, if set X has the values {-10,35,75,100}, then partitioning this set does not provide any additional information, so it's probably better to work with either the mean or the median.

Calculating Interquartile Values

This section shows you how to calculate Q2, followed by Q1, and finally Q3 for a discrete set of integer values. Let's suppose that the set X consists of the values {5, 6, 7, 9, 10, 12, 14}.

The second quartile Q2 is the median value of X, which equals 9. The first quartile Q1 is the median of the data values of X that are less than the second quartile Q2 (i.e., 9), which in turn equals 6. The third quartile Q1 is the median of the data values of X that are greater than the second quartile Q2 (i.e., 9), which in turn equals 12. Therefore, the interquartile term `IQR` equals `Q3-Q1` which equals 6. In tabular form here are the calculated results:

```
Q2 = 9
Q1 = 6
Q3 = 12
IQR = 6
```

A Code Sample With Mean, Median, and Mode

Listing 4.1 displays the contents of the `Python` file `mean_median_mode. py` that shows you how to calculate the mean, median, and mode of a set of numbers.

Listing 4.1: mean_median_mode.py

```python
import statistics as stats

data1  = [1,2,3,4,5]
mean   = stats.mean(data1)
median = stats.median(data1)
mode   = stats.mode(data1)

print("data1: ",data1)
print("mean:   ",mean)
print("median:",median)
print("mode:   ",mode)
print()

data2  = [1,1,1,2,2,2,3,4,5,20]
mean   = stats.mean(data2)
median = stats.median(data2)
mode   = stats.mode(data2)

print("data2: ",data2)
print("mean:   ",mean)
print("median:",median)
print("mode:   ",mode)
```

Listing 4.1 starts with an `import` statement, followed by the variable `data1` that is initialized as a list of integers. The next three code snippets calculate the mean, median, and mode of the values in `data1`, and then display the results.

The second block of code is similar to the previous code block, using the variable `data2` instead of `data1`. Launch the code in Listing 4.1 and you will see the following output:

```
print("data2: ",data2)
data1:   [1, 2, 3, 4, 5]
mean:    3
median: 3
mode:    1

data2:   [1, 1, 1, 2, 2, 2, 3, 4, 5, 20]
mean:    4.1
median: 2.0
mode:    1

data3:   [-2, -1, 1, 2, 30, 40, 50, 2000]
mean:    265
median: 16.0
mode:    -2
```

Here are some suggestions for the use of mean, median, and the mode:

· mean: not skewed interval/ratio
· median: ordinal or skewed interval/ratio
· mode: nominal data

Arithmetic Mean, Harmonic Mean, and Geometric Mean

The *arithmetic mean* is the average value of given data points, which is calculated by dividing the sum of all the observations by the total number of observations. For example, if a and b are two real numbers, then the arithmetic mean is (a+b)/2.

The *harmonic mean* is more complex: it equals the reciprocal of the arithmetic mean of reciprocal values. Given the real numbers a and b, the harmonic mean equals 2/[1/a + 1/b]. Incidentally, the term "harmonic mean" is influenced by the *harmonic series*, which is the sum of the reciprocal of all positive integers: 1/1 + 1/2 + 1/3 + ... Although it's not obvious, the sum of this sequence of numbers is infinite (check online for proof).

The *geometric mean* of two numbers is the square root of the product of those numbers (provided that the product is nonnegative). This can be easily generalized: if the set of k numbers {n1, n2, . . . , nk} has a positive product, then the geometric mean of those numbers is the kth root of n1*n2*...*nk.

As a simple example, suppose that a = 4 and b = 16 (conveniently chosen for the following calculations), then the average of a and b = (4+16)/2 = 10; the harmonic mean of a and b = 1/(1/4 + 16) = 1/(5/16) = 16/5; and the geometric mean of a and b = sqrt(4*16) = sqrt(64) = 8.

THE VARIANCE AND STANDARD DEVIATION

The *variance* of a distribution is E((X_bar - X)**2), which is the mean of the squared difference from the mean. Hence, the variance measures the variability of the numbers from the average value of that same set of numbers. The *standard deviation* is the square root of the variance.

Another way to describe the *variance* is the sum of the squares of the difference between the numbers in X and the mean mu of the set X, divided by the number of values in X, as shown here:

```
variance = [SUM (xi - mu)**2 ] / n
```

For example, if the set X consists of {-10,35,75,100}, then the *mean* equals (-10 + 35 + 75 + 100)/4 = 50, and the variance is computed as follows:

```
variance = [(-10-50)**2 + (35-50)**2 + (75-50)**2 +
(100-50)**2]/4
         = [60**2 + 15**2 + 25**2 + 50**2]/4
         = [3600 + 225 + 625 + 2500]/4
         = 6950/4 = 1,737
```

The standard deviation std is the square root of the variance, as shown here:

```
std = sqrt(1737) = 41.677
```

If the set X consists of {2,2,2,2}, then the *mean* equals (2+2+2+2)/4 = 2, and the variance is computed as follows:

```
variance = [(2-2)**2 + (2-2)**2 + (2-2)**2 +
(2-2)**2]/4
         = [0**2 + 0**2 + 0**2 + 0**2]/4
         = 0
```

The standard deviation `std` is the square root of the variance:

```
std = sqrt(0) = 0
```

Standard Deviation for a Sample Versus a Population

The standard deviation for a sample and the standard deviation for a population contain the quantity n-1 and n, respectively, in the denominator. The reason for this slight difference is that the value n underestimates the true value of the variance and (therefore standard deviation) in the population, which results in a *biased* estimate.

The solution involves replacing n by (n-1) in the denominator to achieve an unbiased estimate. By contrast, notice that the mean of a sample and the mean of a population both contain the quantity n in the denominator.

A Simple Code Sample

Listing 4.2 displays the contents of the Python file `var_pvar_stdev.py` that shows you how to calculate the variance, pvariance, and standard deviation of a set of numbers.

Listing 4.2: var_pvar_stdev.py

```python
import numpy as np
import statistics as stats

values = np.array([1,2,3,4,5,20])
variance  = stats.variance(values)
pvariance = stats.pvariance(values)
stdev     = stats.stdev(values)

print("values:   ",values)
print("pvariance:",pvariance)
print("variance: ",variance)
print("stdev:    ",stdev)
```

Listing 4.2 starts with two `import` statements, followed by a block of code that computes the `variance`, `pvariance`, and `stdev` of the numbers in the `NumPy` array `values`. The next block of code displays the values that were calculated in the first block of code. Launch the code in Listing 4.2 and you will see the following output:

```
values:      [ 1  2  3  4  5 20]
pvariance: 41
variance:  50
stdev:     7.0710678118654755
```

Chebyshev's Inequality

Chebyshev's inequality provides a very simple way to determine the minimum percentage of data that lies within `k` standard deviations. Specifically, this inequality states that for any positive integer `k` greater than 1, the amount of data in a sample that lies within `k` standard deviations is at least `1 - 1/k**2`. This formula is plausible, because larger values of k encompass a larger set of data values, and the quantity `1 - 1/k**2` increases quadratically as the value of k increases linearly. For example, if k = 2, then at least 1 - 1/2**2 = 3/4 of the data must lie within 2 standard deviations; if k = 3, then at least 1 - 1/3**2 = 8/9 of the data must lie within 3 standard deviations.

The interesting part of the term `1 - 1/k**2` is that it has been *mathematically proven* to be true; that is, it's not an empirical or heuristic-based result. An extensive description regarding Chebyshev's inequality (including some advanced mathematical explanations) is here:

https://en.wikipedia.org/wiki/Chebyshev%27s_inequality

SAMPLING TECHNIQUES FOR A POPULATION

This section contains sampling techniques that pertain to creating a sample from a given population. Note that the word *population* specifically refers to the entire set of entities in a given group, such as the population of a country, the people over 65 in the USA, or the number of first year students in a university.

However, in many cases statistical quantities are calculated on samples instead of an entire population. Thus, a sample is (a much smaller) subset of the given population. See the Central Limit Theorem regarding the distribution of the mean of a set of random samples of a population (which need not be a population with a Gaussian distribution).

The following list of bullet items contains common techniques for sampling data from a population:

- cluster Sampling
- convenience Sampling
- quota sampling
- simple random sampling
- stratified sampling
- systematic sampling

One other important point: the population variance is calculated by multiplying the sample variance by $n/(n-1)$, as shown here:

```
population variance = [n/(n-1)]*variance
```

THE CONFUSION MATRIX

A *confusion matrix* provides information that enables you to evaluate classifiers. The confusion matrix is suited for classification tasks: it shows you how many observations were classified by the classification model. In the case of two classes, there are four possibilities:

- true positive
- false positive
- true negative
- false negative

An example of a confusion matrix is shown here, followed by the interpretation of the values in the confusion matrix:

```
[[64  4]
 [ 3 29]]
```

The four values in the preceding 2×2 matrix represent the following quantities:

```
TP = True positive: 64
FP = False positive: 4
TN = True negative: 29
FN = False negative: 3
```

The preceding four quantities occupy the four cells of the following 2×2 binary confusion matrix, which is shown in the following 2×2 grid:

```
TP | FP
-------
FN | TN
```

Another example of a confusion matrix involves three outcomes, which means that the confusion matrix is 3×3 instead of 2×2:

```
[[12  0  2]
 [ 0 15  1]
 [ 2  0  4]]
```

In addition to 2×2 and 3×3 confusion matrices, an nxn confusion matrix is generated when a feature consists of n labels for a given class.

As a practical example, suppose that a dataset that contains clinical trial data for cancer, which involves two classes (healthy and sick). Once again, there are four possible outcomes: true positive, false positive, true negative, and false negative (discussed later). A confusion matrix contains numeric (integer) values for these four quantities. By contrast, linear regression involves terms such as R and R^2 to help you evaluate the accuracy of a model.

Normalized Confusion Matrix

If cm is a confusion matrix, such as the confusion matrix in the previous section, the following code snippet normalizes the values in that matrix:

```
cm = cm.astype('float') / cm.sum(axis=1)[:, np.newaxis]
```

An even simpler way to normalize the values in a confusion matrix cm is shown here, where y_true are the actual labels in a dataset and y_pred are the predicted values that are compared with the actual labels in order to generate a confusion matrix:

```
cm(y_true, y_pred, normalize='all')
```

A third way to normalize a confusion matrix involves scikitplot, as shown here:

```
import scikitplot as skplt
skplt.metrics.plot_confusion_matrix(Y_TRUE,Y_
PRED,normalize=True)
```

The value for normalize in the preceding code snippet might also depend on the version of Python that you have installed on your machine.

Using the confusion matrix from the previous section, the corresponding normalized confusion matrix is here:

```
|0.94117647  0.05882353|
|0.09375     0.90625    |
```

A Python Code Sample of a Confusion Matrix

Listing 4.3 displays the contents of the Python file confusion_matrix.py that shows you how to generate a confusion matrix from a set of numeric data values.

Listing 4.3: confusion_matrix.py

```python
import matplotlib.pyplot as plt
import pandas as pd
import seaborn as sns
from sklearn.metrics import confusion_matrix

data = {'y_true': [1, 0, 0, 1, 0, 1, 0, 0, 1, 0, 1, 0],
        'y_pred': [1, 1, 0, 1, 0, 1, 1, 0, 1, 0, 0, 0]}

print("=> Data Values:")
print(data)
print()

df = pd.DataFrame(data, columns=['y_true','y_pred'])
print("=> DataFrame df:")
print(df)
print()

cm = pd.crosstab(df['y_true'], df['y_pred'],
rownames=['Actual'], colnames=['Predicted'])
print ("=> Confusion matrix:")
print (cm)
print()

cm2 = confusion_matrix(data['y_true'], data['y_pred'],
normalize='all')
print ("=> Normalized Confusion matrix:")
print (cm2)
```

```
sns.heatmap(cm2, annot=True)
plt.show()
```

Listing 4.3 starts with `import` statements and then initializes the variable `data` with a set of 0s and 1s for the `y_true` and the `p_pred` elements. These values were arbitrarily selected, so there is no significance to the chosen values (feel free to specify different values).

The next code block initializes the DataFrame `df` with the values in the variable data, after which the confusion matrix `cm` is generated based the data values in `df`. The confusion matrix is printed, and then a second normalized confusion matrix `cm2` is created and also printed. The last code snippet generates and then displays a `Seaborn` heat map based on the contents of the confusion matrix `cm2`. Launch the code in Listing 4.3 and you will see the following output:

```
=> Data Values:
{'y_true': [0, 1, 0, 1, 0, 1, 1, 1, 1, 1, 1, 1],
  'y_pred': [1, 1, 0, 1, 0, 1, 1, 0, 1, 0, 0, 0]}

=> DataFrame df:
     y_true   y_pred
0        0        1
1        1        1
2        0        0
3        1        1
4        0        0
5        1        1
6        1        1
7        1        0
8        1        1
9        1        0
10       1        0
11       1        0

=> Confusion matrix:
Predicted   0   1
Actual
```

```
0               2   1
1               4   5


=> Normalized Confusion matrix:
[[0.16666667 0.08333333]
 [0.33333333 0.41666667]]
```

Figure 4.1 displays the heat map generated via the `Seaborn` package, using the data from the confusion matrix `cm2`.

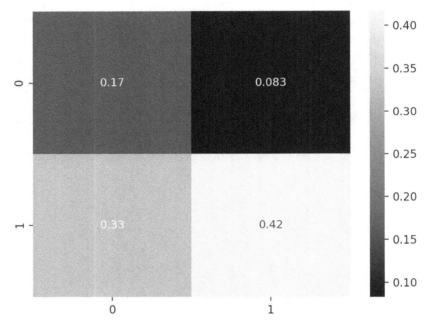

FIGURE 4.1 A best-fitting distribution for a set of random values.

Chapter 5 contains more examples of generating charts and graphs via the `Seaborn` library.

What are TP, FP, FN, and TN?

A binary confusion matrix (also called an error matrix) is a type of contingency table with two rows and two columns that contains the number of false positives, false negatives, true positives, and true negatives. Here is a 2×2 confusion matrix shown again for your convenience:

```
TP | FP
-------
FN | TN
```

The four entries in a 2×2 confusion matrix have labels with the following interpretation:

- `TP: True Positive`
- `FP: False Positive`
- `TN: True Negative`
- `FN: False Negative`

Just to be sure it's clear, the four entries in the confusion matrix can be described as follows:

- `True Positive (TP): Predicted True and actually True`
- `True Negative (TN): Predicted False and actually False`
- `False Positive (FP): Predicted True and actually False`
- `False Negative (FN): Predicted False and actually True`

Hence, the values on the main diagonal of the confusion matrix are *correct* predictions, whereas the off-diagonal values are *incorrect* predictions. In general, a lower `FP` value is better than a `FN` value. For example, an `FP` indicates that a healthy person was incorrectly diagnosed with a disease, whereas an `FN` indicates that an unhealthy person was incorrectly diagnosed as healthy.

Keep in mind that the confusion matrix can be an nxn matrix and not just a 2×2 matrix. For example, if a class has five possible values, then the confusion matrix is a 5×5 matrix, and the numbers on the main diagonal are the "true positive" results.

Type I and Type II Errors

A type I error is a false positive, which means that something is erroneously classified as positive when it's negative. On the other hand, a type II error is a false negative, which means that something is erroneously classified as negative when it's positive.

For example, a woman who is classified as pregnant even though she is not pregnant is a type I error. By contrast, a woman who is classified as *not* pregnant even though she *is* pregnant is a type II error.

As another example, a person who is classified as having cancer even though that person is healthy is a type I error. By contrast, a person who is classified as healthy even though that person has cancer is a type II error.

Based on the preceding examples it's clear that type I and type II are not symmetric in terms of the consequences of their misclassification: sometimes it's a case of life-and-death classification. Among the four possible outcomes, the sequence of outcomes, from best to worst, would be the following:

1. True Negative

2. False Positive

3. True Positive

4. False Negative

Although outcomes 3 and 4 are both highly undesirable, the third option provides accurate information that people can take appropriate action, whereas the fourth option delays the time at which people can take the necessary precautions. Also keep in mind another point regarding a false positive diagnosis: people who are erroneously diagnosed with leukemia or cancer (or some other life-threatening disease) might be needlessly subjected to chemotherapy, which has an unpleasant set of consequences.

Accuracy and Balanced Accuracy

You will often see models evaluated via their accuracy, which is defined by the following formula:

```
accuracy  = % of correct predictions
          = (TP + TN) / total cases


balanced accuracy = (recall+specificity)/2
(intermediate)
```

The formula for balanced accuracy involves `recall` and `specificity`, both of which are discussed later. Although accuracy can be a useful indicator, `accuracy` has limited (and perhaps misleading) value for imbalanced datasets. Accuracy can be an unreliable metric because it yields misleading results in unbalanced datasets. Classes with substantially different sizes are assigned equal importance to both false positive and false negative classifications. For example, declaring cancer as benign is worse than incorrectly informing patients that they are suffering from cancer. Unfortunately, accuracy won't differentiate between these two cases.

A Caveat Regarding Accuracy

Accuracy involves the sum of the true positive and true negative values that are on the main diagonal of the confusion matrix, and disregards type I errors and type II errors (on the off-diagonal of the confusion matrix). Moreover, data belonging to the majority class tend to be given a true classification, and significantly imbalanced datasets tend to skew results toward the majority class.

As a concrete example, consider a dataset that includes 1,000 rows, each representing a person. In total, 1% of the people are sick, which means that 990 people are healthy and 10 people are sick. Now train a model to make predictions on this dataset. The no-code solution is to predict that everyone is healthy, which achieves an accuracy of 99%.

The preceding "no-code solution" is obviously unacceptable because it cannot predict *which* people are sick. Instead of accuracy, consider using one or more of the following:

- Matthews correlation coefficient (CCM)
- Cohen's kappa coefficient
- Student's t-test (for normally distributed data)
- Mann-Whitney U test (for nonnormally distributed data)

Moreover, calculate the values for precision, recall, and F1 scores and compare them with the value of the accuracy, and see how the models react to imbalanced data.

As a rule of thumb: use the accuracy metric when both classes are equally important and 80% are in the majority class.

Recall (Sensitivity), Precision, Specificity, and Prevalence

The definitions of recall, precision, and specificity in the case of a 2x2 confusion matrix are given by the following formulas:

```
recall    = % of correctly identified positive cases
          = TP / (TP + FN)
```

```
precision = % of correct positive predictions
          = TP / (TP + FP).
specificity = TN/[TN+FP]

prevalence  = (TP+FN)/[TP+TN+FP+FN]
```

One way that might help you remember these formulas is to think of their denominators as the sum of the values in columns or rows, as shown here:

- Accuracy = sum-of-main-diagonal/(sum-of-all-terms)
- Precision = TP/(sum-of-row-one)
- Recall   = TP/(sum-of-column-one)
- Specificity = TN/(sum-of-column-two)
- False-positive-rate = TN/(sum-of-column-two)

Recall (also called *sensitivity*) is the proportion of the correctly predicted positive values in the set of actually positively labeled samples: this equals the fraction of the positively labeled samples that were correctly predicted by the model.

The following code snippet shows you how to invoke the `recall_score()` method, which provides a labels parameter for multiclass classification:

```
from sklearn.metrics import recall_score
recall_score(y_true, y_pred,
labels=[1,2],average='micro')
```

The following code snippet shows you how to invoke the `precision_score()` method, which provides a labels parameter for multiclass classification:

```
from sklearn.metrics import precision_score
precision_score(y_true, y_pred,
labels=[1,2],average='micro')
```

Another technique that might help you remember how to calculate precision and recall is to notice that:

1. Both have the same numerator (=TP).

2. The precision denominator is the sum of the first row.

3. The recall denominator is the sum of the first column.

Thus, we can describe accuracy, recall, precision, and specificity as follows:

- Accuracy is the percentage of correctly classified samples of all the samples.
- Recall is the percentages of correctly classified positives of all actual positives.
- Precision is the percentage of correctly classified positives from all predicted positives.
- Specificity is the proportion of negatively labeled samples that were predicted as negative.
- Prevalence is a fraction of total population that is labeled positive.

Precision Versus Recall: How to Decide?

Sometimes precision is more important than recall: of the set of cases that were predicted as valid, how many times were they true? If you are predicting books that are suitable for people under 18, you can afford to reject a few books but cannot afford to accept bad books. If you are predicting thieves in a supermarket, we need a higher value for precision. As you can probably surmise, customer trust will decrease due to false positives.

Just to emphasize what has already been written, *precision* is the proportion of the samples that are actually positive in the set of positively predicted samples, which is expressed informally as:

precision = (# of *correct* positive) / (# of *predicted* positive)

Note: *precision* is important when false positives are more important than false negatives, such as spam detection, and you want to minimize FP.

Recall is the proportion of the samples that are actually positive in the set of actual positive samples, which is expressed informally as:

recall = (# of predicted positive) / (# of actual positive)

Note: *recall* (aka sensitivity) is important when false negatives are more important than false positives, such as cancer detection, and you want to minimize FN.

https://mlu-explain.github.io/precision-recall

TPR, FPR, PV, FDR, and FOR

The quantities TPR, FPR, NPV, FDR, and FOR are additional terms that you might encounter, and they are defined in this section.

TPR = true positive rate
TPR = proportion of positively labeled samples that are *correctly* predicted positive
```
TPR = TP/[TP+FN] = TP/(sum-of-column-one)
```

FPR = false positive rate
FPR = proportion of negatively labeled samples that are *incorrectly* predicted positive
```
FPR = FP/[TN+FP] = FP/(sum-of-column-two)
```

NPV = Negative Predictive Value or NPV
NPV = proportion of negatively labeled samples that are *correctly* predicted negative
```
NPV = TN/[TN+FN] = TN/(sum-of-row-two)
```

```
FDR = false discovery rate = 1 - PPV = FP/[TP+FP] = FP/(sum-of-row-one)
```

FOR = false omission rate
```
FOR = 1 - NPV = FN/[TN+FN] = FN/(sum-of-row-two)
```
The following bullet list contains the values of the quantities TPR, FPR, NPV, FDR, and FOR in a single bullet list:

- `TPR = TP/(sum-of-column-one)`
- `FPR = FP/(sum-of-column-two)`
- `NPV = TN/(sum-of-row-two)`
- `FDR = FP/(sum-of-row-one)`
- `FOR = FN/(sum-of-row-two)`

In a previous section, you learned about a confusion matrix, and the following output shows you the calculated values for precision, recall, F1-score, and accuracy that can be generated via `scikit-learn`:

```
from sklearn.metrics import confusion_matrix,
classification_report
# displays values for precision/recall/f1-score/
support:
print(classification_report(y_test, y_pred))
```

	precision	recall	f1-score	support
0	0.96	0.94	0.95	68
1	0.88	0.91	0.89	32

			0.93	100
accuracy			0.93	100
macro avg	0.92	0.92	0.92	100
weighted avg	0.93	0.93	0.93	100

CALCULATING EXPECTED VALUES

Consider the following scenario involving a well-balanced coin: whenever a head appears, you earn $1 and whenever a tail appears, you earn $1 dollar. If you toss the coin 100 times, how much money do you expect to earn? Since you will earn $1 regardless of the outcome, the expected value (in fact, the guaranteed value) is 100.

Now consider this scenario: whenever a head appears, you earn $1 and whenever a tail appears, you earn 0 dollars. If you toss the coin 100 times, how much money do you expect to earn? You probably determined the value 50 (which is the correct answer) by making a quick mental calculation. The more formal derivation of the value of E (the expected earning) is here:

```
E = 100 *[1 * 0.5 + 0 * 0.5] = 100 * 0.5 = 50
```

The quantity **1** * 0.5 + **0** * 0.5 is the amount of money you expected to collect during each coin toss (half the time you collect $1 and half the time you collect 0 dollars), and multiplying this number by 100 is the expected amount collected after 100 coin tosses. Also note that you might never collect $50: the actual amount that you collect can be any integer between 1 and 100 inclusive.

As another example, suppose that you collect $3 whenever a head appears, and you *lose* $1.50 dollars whenever a tail appears. Then the expected amount collected E after 100 coin tosses is shown here:

```
E = 100 *[3 * 0.5 - 1.5 * 0.5] = 100 * 1.5 = 150
```

We can generalize the preceding calculations as follows. Let P = {p1, ..., pn} be a probability distribution, which means that the values in P are nonnegative and their sum equals 1. In addition, let R = {R1, ..., Rn} be a set of rewards, where reward Ri is received with probability pi. Then the expected value E after N trials is shown here:

```
          n
E = N * [SUM pi*Ri]
        i=0
```

In the case of a single balanced die, we have the following probabilities:

```
p(1) = 1/6
p(2) = 1/6
p(3) = 1/6
p(4) = 1/6
p(5) = 1/6
p(6) = 1/6
P = { 1/6, 1/6, 1/6, 1/6, 1/6, 1/6}
```

As a simple example, suppose that the earnings are {3, 0, -1, 2, 4, -1} when the values 1,2,3,4,5,6, respectively, appear when tossing the single die. Then after 100 trials our expected earnings are calculated as follows:

```
E = 100 * [3 + 0 + -1 + 2 + 4 + -1]/6 = 100 * 3/6 = 50
```

In the case of two balanced dice, we have the following probabilities of rolling 2, 3, ... , or 12:

```
p(2) = 1/36
p(3) = 2/36
...
p(12) = 1/36
P = {1/36,2/36,3/36,4/36,5/36,6/36,5/36,4/36,3/36,
2/36,1/36}
```

Random Variables and Expected Values

This section involves an understanding of the notion of a random variable, which is discussed earlier in this chapter.

Suppose that X is a random variable, such as the outcome of tossing a fair coin that has two possible outcomes. If tossing a heads has reward R1 and tossing tails has a reward R2, then the expected value E(X) is shown here:

```
E(X) = (1/2)*R1 + (1/2)*R2 = (R1+R2)/2.
```

In addition, if c is a constant and Y is another random variable, then the following are true:

```
E(X+c) = E(X) + c
E(X*c) = E(X) * c
E(X+Y) = E(X) + E(Y)
```

Moreover, if `x_bar` is the mean of a sample of size n from a population, then `x_bar` is a random variable with the following properties:

```
E(x_bar) = x_bar
var(x_bar) = var(X)/n
```

SUMMARY

This chapter started with a brief description regarding the need for statistics, followed by some well-known terminology, and then the concept of a random variable, which can be either continuous or discrete.

Then you learned about mean, median, mode, variance, and standard deviation, along with Chebyshev's inequality, dispersion, and sampling techniques. Next, you saw how to detect normally distributed data, such as D'Agostino's test, Pearson's correlation coefficient, and augmented Dickey-Fuller.

You also learned about several continuous probability distributions, such as chi-square, Gaussian, and uniform distribution, followed by some discrete probability distributions, such as Bernoulli, binomial, exponential, and Poisson distribution.

In addition, you saw how to compute metrics for linear regression, including MAE, MSE, RMSE, and MMR, followed by concepts such as the CLT, causality and the contrapositive, and statistical inferences.

In the final portion of this chapter, you learned about the confusion matrix for machine learning classification algorithms, and a description of type I errors, type II errors, and the metrics accuracy, precision, and recall. You also learned about the ROC curve and the AUC curve. Lastly, you learned about the F1 score and related scores, such as F2, and F3 that are useful for classification algorithms.

REFERENCES

Pinkstone, J. (2022). Why packing your diet with vegetables may note guarantee a healthy heart. *The Telegraph. https://www.yahoo.com/news/why-packing-diet-vegetables-may-205810092.html*

MATPLOTLIB AND SEABORN

This chapter introduces data visualization, along with a collection of `Python`-based code samples that use `Matplotlib` to render charts and graphs. In addition, this chapter contains visualization code samples that combine `Pandas` and `Matplotlib`.

The first part of this chapter briefly discusses data visualization, with a short list of some data visualization tools, and a list of various types of visualization (bar graphs, pie charts, and so forth). This section also contains a very short introduction to `Matplotlib`, followed by short code samples that display the available styles in colors in `Matplotlib`.

The second part of this chapter contains an assortment of `Python` code samples that use `Matplotlib` in order to render horizontal lines, slanted lines, and parallel lines. This section also shows you how to render a grid of points in several ways.

The third section contains examples of rendering charts and graphs in `Matplotlib`, which includes histograms, bar charts, pie charts, and heat maps. The fourth section contains code samples that use the `Python` open-source libraries `SweetViz` and `Skimpy`. The final section of this chapter introduces `Seaborn` for data visualization, along with an assortment of charts and graphs.

WHAT IS DATA VISUALIZATION?

Data visualization refers to presenting data in a graphical manner, such as bar charts, line graphs, heat maps, and many other specialized representations. As you probably know, Big Data comprises massive amounts of data, which leverages data visualization tools to assist in making better decisions.

A key role for good data visualization is to tell a meaningful story, which in turn focuses on useful information that resides in datasets that can contain many data points (i.e., billions of rows of data). Another aspect of data visualization is its effectiveness: how well does it convey the trends that might exist in the dataset?

There are many open-source data visualization tools available, some of which are listed here (many others are available):

- Matplotlib
- Seaborn
- Bokeh
- YellowBrick
- Tableau
- D3.js (JavaScript and SVG)

Incidentally, in case you have not already done so, it would be helpful to install the following `Python` libraries (using `pip3`) on your computer so that you can launch the following code samples that appear in this chapter:

```
pip3 install matplotlib
pip3 install seaborn
pip3 install bokeh
```

Types of Data Visualization

Bar graphs, line graphs, and pie charts are common ways to present data, and yet many other types exist, some of which are listed below:

- 2D/3D Area Chart
- Bar Chart
- Gantt Chart
- Heat Map
- Histogram
- Polar Area
- Scatter Plot (2D or 3D)
- Timeline

The `Python` code samples in the next several sections illustrate how to perform visualization via rudimentary APIs from `matplotlib`.

WHAT IS MATPLOTLIB?

Matplotlib is a plotting library that supports NumPy, SciPy, and toolkits such as wxPython (among others). Matplotlib supports only version 3 of Python: support for version 2 of Python was available only through 2020. Matplotlib is a multiplatform library that is built on NumPy arrays.

The plotting-related code samples in this chapter use pyplot, which is a Matplotlib module that provides a MATLAB-like interface. Here is an example of using pyplot to plot a smooth curve based on negative powers of Euler's constant e:

```
import matplotlib.pyplot as plt
import numpy as np

lin_data = np.linspace(0, 10, 100)
exp_data = np.exp(-lin_data)
plt.plot(lin_data, exp_data)
plt.show()
```

Keep in mind that the code samples that plot line segments assume that you are familiar with the equation of a (nonvertical) line in the plane: $y = m*x + b$, where m is the slope and b is the y-intercept.

Furthermore, some code samples use NumPy APIs such as np.linspace(), np.array(), np.random.rand(), and np.ones() that are discussed in Chapter 3, so you can refresh your memory regarding these APIs.

MATPLOTLIB STYLES

Listing 5.1 displays the contents of mpl_styles.py that illustrates how to plot a pie chart in Matplotlib.

Listing 5.1: mpl_styles.py

```
import matplotlib.pyplot as plt

print("plt.style.available:")
styles = plt.style.available
```

```
for style in styles:
  print("style:",style)
```

Listing 5.1 contains an `import` statement, followed by the variable `styles` that is initialized with the set of available styles in `Matplotlib`. The final portion of Listing 5.1 contains a loop that iterates through the values in the `styles` variable. Launch the code in Listing 5.1 and you will see the following output:

```
plt.style.available:
style: Solarize_Light2
style: _classic_test_patch
style: bmh
style: classic
style: dark_background
style: fast
style: fivethirtyeight
style: ggplot
style: grayscale
style: seaborn
style: seaborn-bright
style: seaborn-colorblind
style: seaborn-dark
style: seaborn-dark-palette
style: seaborn-darkgrid
style: seaborn-deep
style: seaborn-muted
style: seaborn-notebook
style: seaborn-paper
style: seaborn-pastel
style: seaborn-poster
style: seaborn-talk
style: seaborn-ticks
style: sea born-white
style: seaborn-whitegrid
style: tableau-colorblind10
```

DISPLAY ATTRIBUTE VALUES

Listing 5.2 displays the contents of `mat_attrib_values.py` that displays the attribute values of an object in `Matplotlib` (subplots are discussed later in this chapter).

Listing 5.2: mat_attrib_values.py

```
import matplotlib.pyplot as plt

fig, ax = plt.subplots()

print("=> attribute values:")
print(plt.getp(fig))
```

Listing 5.2 contains an `import` statement, followed by the variables `fig` and `ax` that are initialized by invoking the `subplots()` method of the `plt` class. The next block of code prints the attribute values in `fig` by invoking the `plt.getp()` method. Launch the code in Listing 5.2 and you will see the following output:

```
=> attribute values:
    agg_filter = None
    alpha = None
    animated = False
    axes = [<AxesSubplot:>]
    children = [<matplotlib.patches.Rectangle object at
    0x11c34f0...
    clip_box = None
    clip_on = True
    clip_path = None
    constrained_layout = False
    constrained_layout_pads = (0.04167, 0.04167, 0.02,
    0.02)
    contains = None
    default_bbox_extra_artists = [<AxesSubplot:>,
    <matplotlib.spines.Spine object a...
    dpi = 100.0
```

```
edgecolor = (1.0, 1.0, 1.0, 1.0)
facecolor = (1.0, 1.0, 1.0, 1.0)
figheight = 4.8
figure = None
figwidth = 6.4
frameon = True
gid = None
in_layout = True
label =
path_effects = []
picker = None
rasterized = None
size_inches = [6.4 4.8]
sketch_params = None
snap = None
tight_layout = False
transform = IdentityTransform()
transformed_clip_path_and_affine = (None, None)
url = None
visible = True
window_extent = TransformedBbox(      Bbox(x0=0.0,
y0=0.0, x1=6.4, ...
zorder = 0
None
```

COLOR VALUES IN MATPLOTLIB

Listing 5.3 displays the contents of mat_colors.py that displays the colors that are available in Matplotlib.

Listing 5.3: mat_colors.py

```
import matplotlib
import matplotlib.pyplot as plt

colors = plt.colormaps()
```

```
col_count=5
idx=0
for color in colors:
  if(color.endswith("_r") == False):
    print(color," ",end="")
    idx += 1
    if(idx % col_count == 0):
      print()
print()
print("=> color count:",idx)
```

Listing 5.3 contains two `import` statements, after which the variable `colors` is initialized with the list of available colors. The next portion of Listing 5.3 contains a loop that iterates through the `colors` variable, and prints the value of each color, provided that it does not have the suffix "_r" in its name. A newline is printed each time that five colors have been printed. Launch the code in Listing 5.3 and you will see the following output:

```
Accent   Blues   BrBG   BuGn   BuPu
CMRmap   Dark2   GnBu   Greens   Greys
OrRd   Oranges   PRGn   Paired   Pastel1
Pastel2   PiYG   PuBu   PuBuGn   PuOr
PuRd   Purples   RdBu   RdGy   RdPu
RdYlBu   RdYlGn   Reds   Set1   Set2
Set3   Spectral   Wistia   YlGn   YlGnBu
YlOrBr   YlOrRd   afmhot   autumn   binary
bone   brg   bwr   cividis   cool
coolwarm   copper   cubehelix   flag   gist_earth
gist_gray   gist_heat   gist_ncar   gist_rainbow   gist_
stern
gist_yarg   gnuplot   gnuplot2   gray   hot
hsv   inferno   jet   magma   nipy_spectral
ocean   pink   plasma   prism   rainbow
seismic   spring   summer   tab10   tab20
tab20b   tab20c   terrain   turbo   twilight
twilight_shifted   viridis   winter
=> color count: 83
```

Now let's proceed to the next section that contains a fast-paced set of basic code samples that display various types of line segments.

CUBED NUMBERS IN MATPLOTLIB

Listing 5.4 displays the contents of cubed_numbers.py that illustrates how to plot a set of points using Matplotlib.

Listing 5.4: cubed_numbers.py

```
import matplotlib.pyplot as plt

plt.plot([1, 2, 3, 4], [1, 8, 27, 64])

plt.axis([0, 5, 0, 70])
plt.xlabel("Integers (1-4)")
plt.ylabel("Cubed Integers")
plt.show()
```

Listing 5.4 plots a set of integer-valued points whose x-coordinate is between 1 and 4 inclusive and whose y-coordinate is the cube of the corresponding x-coordinate. The code sample also labels the horizontal axis and the vertical axis. Figure 5.1 displays these points in Listing 5.4.

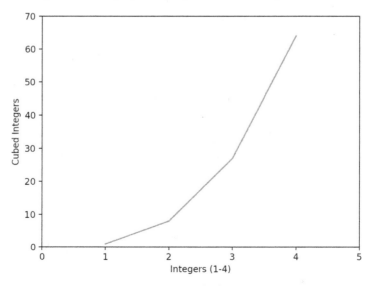

FIGURE 5.1 A graph of cubed numbers.

HORIZONTAL LINES IN MATPLOTLIB

Listing 5.5 displays the contents of hlines1.py that illustrates how to plot horizontal lines using Matplotlib. Recall that the equation of a nonvertical line in the 2D plane is y = m*x + b, where m is the slope of the line and b is the y-intercept of the line.

Listing 5.5: hlines1.py

```python
import numpy as np
import matplotlib.pyplot as plt

# top line
x1 = np.linspace(-5,5,num=200)
y1 = 4 + 0*x1

# middle line
x2 = np.linspace(-5,5,num=200)
y2 = 0 + 0*x2

# bottom line
x3 = np.linspace(-5,5,num=200)
y3 = -3 + 0*x3

plt.axis([-5, 5, -5, 5])
plt.plot(x1,y1)
plt.plot(x2,y2)
plt.plot(x3,y3)
plt.show()
```

Listing 5.5 uses the np.linspace() API in order to generate a list of 200 equally spaced numbers for the horizontal axis, all of which are between -5 and 5. The three lines defined via the variables y1, y2, and y3, are defined in terms of the variables x1, x2, and x3, respectively.

Figure 5.2 displays three horizontal line segments whose equations are contained in Listing 5.5.

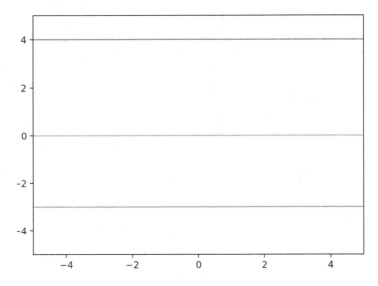

FIGURE 5.2 A graph of three horizontal line segments.

SLANTED LINES IN MATPLOTLIB

Listing 5.6 displays the contents of `diagonallines.py` that illustrates how to plot slanted lines.

Listing 5.6: diagonallines.py

```
import matplotlib.pyplot as plt
import numpy as np

x1 = np.linspace(-5,5,num=200)
y1 = x1

x2 = np.linspace(-5,5,num=200)
y2 = -x2
```

```
plt.axis([-5, 5, -5, 5])
plt.plot(x1,y1)
plt.plot(x2,y2)
plt.show()
```

Listing 5.6 defines two lines using the technique that you saw in Listing 5.5, except that these two lines define `y1 = x1` and `y2 = -x2`, which produces slanted lines instead of horizontal lines.

Figure 5.3 displays two slanted line segments whose equations are defined in Listing 5.6.

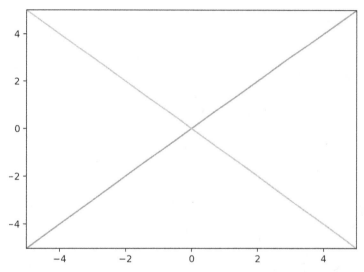

FIGURE 5.3 A graph of two slanted line segments.</fn>

PARALLEL SLANTED LINES IN `MATPLOTLIB`

If two lines in the Euclidean plane have the same slope, then they are parallel. Listing 5.7 displays the contents of `parallellines1.py` that illustrates how to plot parallel slanted lines.

Listing 5.7: parallellines1.py

```
import matplotlib.pyplot as plt
import numpy as np

# lower line
x1 = np.linspace(-5,5,num=200)
y1 = 2*x1

# upper line
x2 = np.linspace(-5,5,num=200)
y2 = 2*x2 + 3

# horizontal axis
x3 = np.linspace(-5,5,num=200)
y3 = 0*x3 + 0

# vertical axis
plt.axvline(x=0.0)

plt.axis([-5, 5, -10, 10])
plt.plot(x1,y1)
plt.plot(x2,y2)
plt.plot(x3,y3)
plt.show()
```

Listing 5.7 defines three lines using the technique that you saw in Listing 5.6, where these three lines are slanted and also parallel to each other.

Figure 5.4 displays two slanted and also parallel line segments whose equations are defined in Listing 5.4.

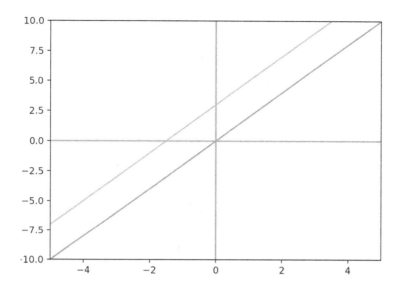

FIGURE 5.4 A graph of two slanted parallel line segments.

LINES AND LABELED VERTICES IN `MATPLOTLIB`

Listing 5.8 displays the contents of `multi_lines.py` that illustrates how to plot multiple line segments with labeled vertices.

Listing 5.8: multi_lines.py

```
import matplotlib.pyplot as plt

x_coord = [ 50, 300, 175, 50]
y_coord = [ 50, 50,  150, 50]
plt.plot(x_coord,y_coord)
plt.scatter(x_coord,y_coord)

for x,y in zip(x_coord,y_coord):
   plt.text(x,y,'Coord ({x},{y})'.format(x=x,y=y))
```

```
x_coord = [ 175,  300,   50,  175]
y_coord = [  50,  150,  150,   50]
plt.plot(x_coord,y_coord)
plt.scatter(x_coord,y_coord)

for x,y in zip(x_coord,y_coord):
    plt.text(x,y,'Coord ({x},{y})'.format(x=x,y=y))
plt.show()
```

Listing 5.8 defines the NumPy variable points that defines a 2D list of points with three rows and four columns. The Pyplot API plot() uses the points variable to display a grid-like pattern. Figure 5.5 displays a grid of points as defined in Listing 5.9.

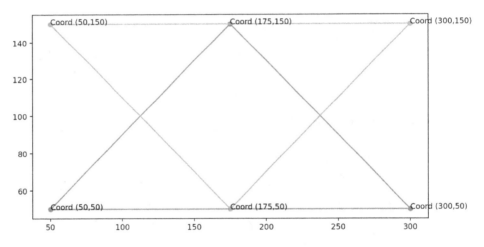

FIGURE 5.5 Lines and labeled vertices.

A DOTTED GRID IN MATPLOTLIB

Listing 5.9 displays the contents of plotdottedgrid1.py that illustrates how to plot a "dotted" grid pattern.

Listing 5.9: plotdottedgrid1.py

```
import numpy as np
import pylab
from itertools import product
import matplotlib.pyplot as plt

fig = pylab.figure()
ax = fig.add_subplot(1,1,1)

ax.grid(which='major', axis='both', linestyle='--')

[line.set_zorder(3) for line in ax.lines]
fig.show() # to update

plt.gca().xaxis.grid(True)
plt.show()
```

Listing 5.9 is similar to the code in Listing 5.8 in that both of them plot a grid-like pattern; however, the former renders a "dotted" grid pattern whereas the latter renders a "dotted" grid pattern by specifying the value '--' for the linestyle parameter.

The next portion of Listing 5.9 invokes the set_zorder() method that controls which items are displayed on top of other items, such as dots on top of lines, or vice versa. The final portion of Listing 5.9 invokes the gca(). xaxis.grid(True) chained methods to display the vertical grid lines.

You can also use the plt.style directive to specify a style for figures. The following code snippet specifies the classic style of Matplotlib:

```
plt.style.use('classic')
```

Figure 5.6 displays a "dashed" grid pattern based on the code in Listing 5.10.

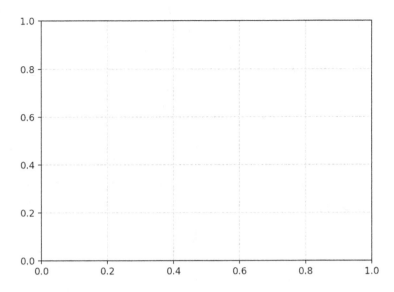

FIGURE 5.6 A "dashed" grid pattern.

LINES IN A GRID IN MATPLOTLIB

Listing 5.10 displays the contents of `plotlinegrid2.py` that illustrates how to plot lines in a grid.

Listing 5.10: plotlinegrid2.py

```
import numpy as np
import pylab
from itertools import product
import matplotlib.pyplot as plt

fig = plt.figure()
graph = fig.add_subplot(1,1,1)
graph.grid(which='major', linestyle='-',
linewidth='0.5', color='red')
```

```
x1 = np.linspace(-5,5,num=200)
y1 = 1*x1
graph.plot(x1,y1, 'r-o')

x2 = np.linspace(-5,5,num=200)
y2 = -x2
graph.plot(x2,y2, 'b-x')

fig.show() # to update
plt.show()
```

Listing 5.10 defines the NumPy variable points that defines a 2D list of points with three rows and four columns. The Pyplot API plot() uses the points variable to display a grid-like pattern.

Figure 5.7 displays a set of "dashed" line segments whose equations are contained in Listing 5.10.

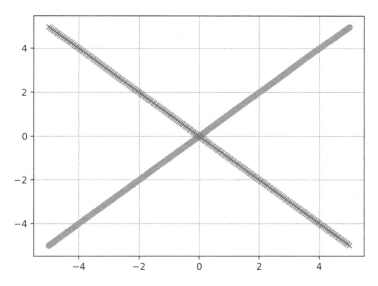

FIGURE 5.7 A grid of line segments.

TWO LINES AND A LEGEND IN MATPLOTLIB

Listing 5.11 displays the contents of `plotgrid2.py` that illustrates how to display a colored grid.

Listing 5.11: two_lines_legend.py

```
import matplotlib.pyplot as plt

# FIRST PLOT:
vals_x = [91,93,95,96,97,98,99,99,104,115]
vals_y = [1500,2000,3000,2500,1200,1500,2900,3200,5200
,6500]
plt.plot(vals_x, vals_y) # alternate style
#plt.plot(vals_x, vals_y, label='First List')

# SECOND PLOT:
vals_x2 = [91,93,95,96,97,98,99,99,104,115]
vals_y2 = [1005,1006,1007,1008,1009,2031,3100,2033,303
4,4035]
plt.plot(vals_x2, vals_y2)
#plt.plot(vals_x2, vals_y2, label='Second List') #
alternate style

# generate line plot:
plt.plot(vals_x, vals_y)
plt.title("Random Pairs of Numbers")
plt.xlabel("Random X Values")
plt.ylabel("Random Y Values")
plt.legend(['First List','Second List'])
#plt.legend() # alternate style
plt.show()
```

Listing 5.11 defines the NumPy variable `data` that defines a 2D set of points with ten rows and ten columns. The Pyplot API `plot()` uses the `data` variable to display a colored grid-like pattern. Figure 5.8 displays a colored grid whose equations are contained in Listing 5.11.

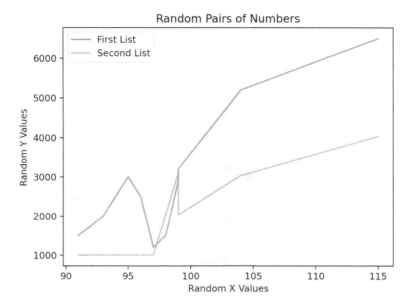

FIGURE 5.8 Two lines and a legend.

LOADING IMAGES IN MATPLOTLIB

Listing 5.12 displays the contents of load_images2.py that illustrates how to display an image.

Listing 5.12: load_images2.py

```
from sklearn.datasets import load_digits
from matplotlib import pyplot as plt

digits = load_digits()
#set interpolation='none'

fig = plt.figure(figsize=(3, 3))
plt.imshow(digits['images'][66], cmap="gray",
interpolation='none')
plt.show()
```

Listing 5.12 starts with two `import` statements and then the `digits` variable is initialized with the contents of the `digits` dataset. The next portion of Listing 5.12 displays the contents of one of the images in the `digits` dataset. Launch the code in Listing 5.12 and you will see the image in Figure 5.9.

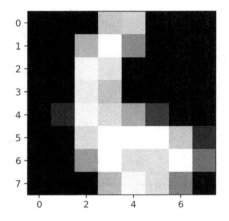

FIGURE 5.9 Loading an image in Matplotlib.

A SET OF LINE SEGMENTS IN MATPLOTLIB

Listing 5.15 displays the contents of `line_segments.py` that illustrates how to plot a set of connected line segments in `Matplotlib`.

Listing 5.15: line_segments.py

```
import numpy as np
import matplotlib.pyplot as plt

x = [7,11,13,15,17,19,23,29,31,37]

plt.plot(x) # OR: plt.plot(x, 'ro-') or bo
plt.ylabel('Height')
plt.xlabel('Weight')
plt.show()
```

Listing 5.15 defines the array x that contains a hard-coded set of values. The `Pyplot` API `plot()` uses the variable x to display a set of connected line segments. Figure 5.10 displays the result of launching the code in Listing 5.16.

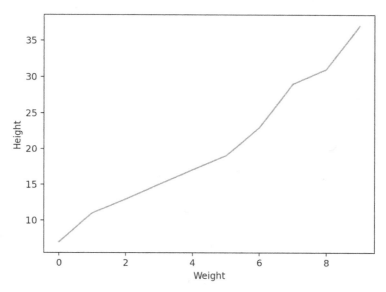

FIGURE 5.10 A set of connected line segments.

PLOTTING MULTIPLE LINES IN MATPLOTLIB

Listing 5.16 displays the contents of `plt_array2.py` that illustrates the ease with which you can plot multiple lines in `Matplotlib`.

Listing 5.16: plt_array2.py

```
import matplotlib.pyplot as plt

x = [7,11,13,15,17,19,23,29,31,37]
data = [[8, 4, 1], [5, 3, 3], [6, 0, 2], [1, 7, 9]]
plt.plot(data, 'd-')
plt.show()
```

Listing 5.16 defines the array `data` that contains a hard-coded set of values. The `Pyplot` API `plot()` uses the variable `data` to display a line segment. Figure 5.11 displays multiple lines based on the code in Listing 5.16.

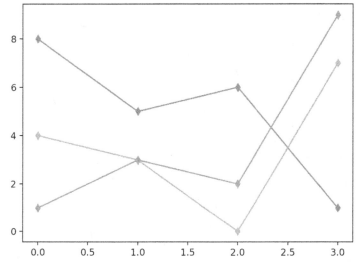

FIGURE 5.11 Multiple lines in Matplotlib.

Now let's look at a simple dataset consisting of discrete data points, which is the topic of the next section.

A HISTOGRAM IN MATPLOTLIB

Listing 5.18 displays the contents of `histogram1.py` that illustrates how to plot a histogram using `Matplotlib`.

Listing 5.18: histogram1.py

```
import matplotlib.pyplot as plt

x = [1, 2, 3, 4, 5, 6, 7, 4]

plt.hist(x, bins = [1, 2, 3, 4, 5, 6, 7])
plt.title("Histogram")
```

```
plt.legend(["bar"])
plt.show()
```

Listing 5.18 is straightforward: the variable x is initialized as a set of numbers, followed by a block of code that renders a histogram based on the data in the variable x. Launch the code in Listing 5.18 and you will see the histogram that is shown in Figure 5.12.

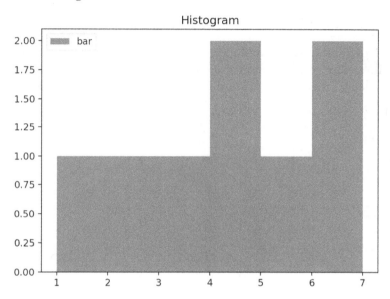

FIGURE 5.12 A histogram based on random values.

PLOT BAR CHARTS

Listing 5.21 displays the contents of barchart1.py that illustrates how to plot a bar chart in Matplotlib.

Listing 5.21: barchart1.py

```
import matplotlib.pyplot as plt

x = [3, 1, 3, 12, 2, 4, 4]
y = [3, 2, 1, 4, 5, 6, 7]
```

```
plt.bar(x, y)

plt.title("Bar Chart")
plt.legend(["bar"])
plt.show()
```

Listing 5.21 contains an `import` statement followed by the variables x and y that are initialized as a list of numbers. Next, the bar chart is generated by invoking the `bar()` method of the `plt` class. The final block of code sets the title and legend for the bar chart and then displays the bar chart. Launch the code in Listing 5.21 and you will see the pie chart displayed in Figure 5.13.

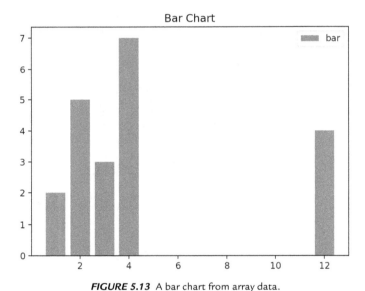

FIGURE 5.13 A bar chart from array data.

Listing 5.22 displays the contents of `barchart2.py` that illustrates how to plot a bar chart in `Matplotlib`.

Listing 5.22: barchart2.py

```
import matplotlib.pyplot as plt

plt.bar([0.25,1.25,2.25,3.25,4.25],
```

```
        [50,40,70,80,20],
        label="GDP1",width=.5)

plt.bar([.75,1.75,2.75,3.75,4.75],
        [80,20,20,50,60],
        label="GDP2", color='r',width=.5)

plt.legend()
plt.xlabel('Months')
plt.ylabel('GDP (Billion Euross)')
plt.title('Bar Chart Comparison')
```

Listing 5.22 contains an `import` statement followed by the definition of two bar charts that are displayed in a side-by-side manner. Notice that the definition of each bar chart involves specifying the x and y (even though they are not explicitly included), followed by a value for the `label` and `width` arguments. The final block of code sets the legend and labels for the horizontal and vertical axes. Launch the code in Listing 5.22 and you will see the pie chart displayed in Figure 5.14.

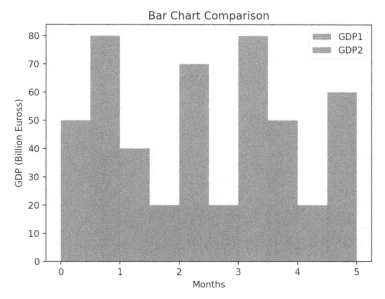

FIGURE 5.14 Two bar charts.

PLOT A PIE CHART

Listing 5.23 displays the contents of `piechart1.py` that illustrates how to plot a pie chart in `Matplotlib`.

Listing 5.23: piechart1.py

```
import numpy as np

# data to display on plots
x = [1, 2, 3, 4]

# explode the first wedge:
e =(0.1, 0, 0, 0)

plt.pie(x, explode = e)
plt.title("Pie chart")
plt.show()
```

Listing 5.23 contains an `import` statement followed by the variables x and e that are initialized as a list of numbers. The values for x are used to calculate the relative size of each "slice" of the pie chart, and the values for the variable e indicate that the first pie slice is "exploded" slightly (indicated by the value 0.1 in e), Launch the code in Listing 5.23 and you will see the pie chart displayed in Figure 5.15.

Pie chart

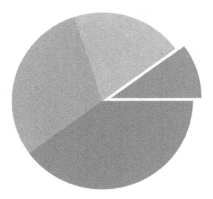

FIGURE 5.15 A basic pie chart.

HEAT MAPS

Listing 5.24 displays the contents of `heatmap1.py` that illustrates how to render a heat map based on random data values.

Listing 5.24: heatmap1.py

```
import numpy as np

data = np.random.random((16, 16))
plt.imshow(data, cmap='tab20_r',
interpolation='nearest')
plt.show()
```

Listing 5.24 contains an `import` statement, followed by the variable `data` that is initialized as a 16x16 matrix of random values. The next code snippet renders the heat map, and the final code snippet displays the heat map. Launch the code in Listing 5.24 and you will see the following output:

```
data.head():
year    1949  1950  1951  1952  1953  1954  1955  1956
        1957  1958  1959  1960

month
Jan     112   115   145   171   196   204   242   284
        315   340   360   417

Feb     118   126   150   180   196   188   233   277
        301   318   342   391

Mar     132   141   178   193   236   235   267   317
        356   362   406   419

Apr     129   135   163   181   235   227   269   313
        348   348   396   461

May     121   125   172   183   229   234   270   318
        355   363   420   472
```

In addition to the preceding data, you will also see the image that is shown in Figure 5.16.

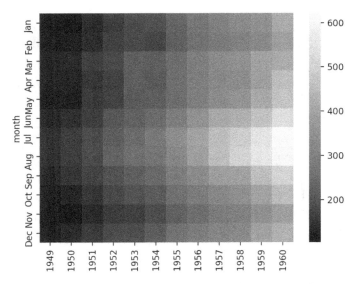

FIGURE 5.16 A heat map from random data.

SAVE PLOT AS A PNG FILE

Listing 5.25 displays the contents of `matplot2png.py` that shows you how to save a graphics image as a PNG file.

Listing 5.25: matplot2png.py

```
import matplotlib.pyplot as plt
import numpy as np

outfile="graph1.png"

plt.figure()
plt.plot(range(6))

fig, ax = plt.subplots()
```

```
ax.plot([2, 3, 4, 5, 5, 6, 6],
        [5, 7, 1, 3, 4, 6 ,8])

ax.plot([1, 2, 3, 4, 5],
        [2, 3, 4, 5, 6])

x = np.linspace(0, 12, 100)
plt.plot(np.sin(x))
plt.plot(np.linspace(-4,4,50))

plt.savefig(outfile, dpi=300)
```

Listing 5.25 contains `import` statements, followed by the variable `out-file` that is initialized with the name of the PNG file that will be saved to the file system. The contents of the PNG file consist of a sine wave and a set of line segments. Launch the code in Listing 5.25 and you will see the image that is shown in Figure 5.17.

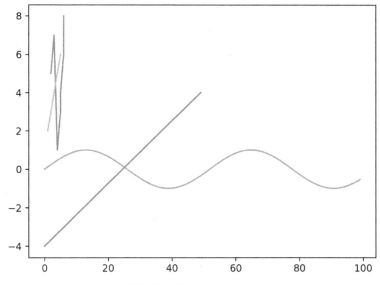

FIGURE 5.17 A random image.

WORKING WITH SWEETVIZ

SweetViz is an open-source Python module that generates remarkably detailed visualizations in the form of HTML Web pages based on literally five lines of Python code.

As an illustration of the preceding statement, Listing 5.26 shows the contents of sweetviz1.py that generates a visualization of various aspects of the Iris dataset that is available in Scikit-learn.

Listing 5.26: sweetviz1.py

```
import sweetviz as sv
import seaborn as sns

df = sns.load_dataset('iris')
report = sv.analyze(df)
report.show_html()
```

Listing 5.26 starts with two import statements, followed by an initialization of the variable df with the contents of the Iris dataset. The next code snippet initializes the variable report as the result of invoking the analyze() method in SweetViz, followed by a code snippet that generates an HTML Web page with the result of the analysis.

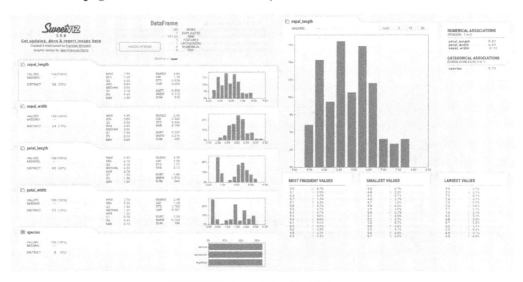

FIGURE 5.18 An analysis of the Iris dataset.

Launch the code from the command line and you will see a new HTML Web page called SWEETVIZ_REPORT.html in the same directory. Figure 5.18 displays the contents of the Web page SWEETVIZ_REPORT.html.

WORKING WITH SKIMPY

Skimpy is an open-source Python module that generates an analysis of a dataset directly from the command line: no Python code is required. Install Skimpy with the following command:

```
pip3 install skimpy
```

Launch the following command to analysis the Titanic dataset (or a dataset of your own choice) that redirects the output to a text file (the latter is optional):

```
skimpy titanic.csv >titanic_out.txt
```

Figure 5.19 displays the contents of the generated output.

```
─────────── skimpy summary ───────────
      Data Summary                Data Types

  ┌─────────────────┬────────┐  ┌─────────────┬───────┐
  │ dataframe    .   │ Values │  │ Column Type │ Count │
  ├─────────────────┼────────┤  ├─────────────┼───────┤
  │ Number of rows   │ 891    │  │ object      │ 7     │
  │ Number of columns│ 15     │  │ int64       │ 4     │
  └─────────────────┴────────┘  │ float64     │ 2     │
                                │ bool        │ 2     │
                                └─────────────┴───────┘

                          number
```

	missing	complete rate	mean	sd	p0	p25	p75	p100	hist
survived	0	1.0	0.38	0.49	0.0	0.0	1.0	1.0	
pclass	0	1.0	2.31	0.84	1.0	2.0	3.0	3.0	
age	177	0.8	29.7	14.53	0.42	20.12	38.0	80.0	
sibsp	0	1.0	0.52	1.1	0.0	0.0	1.0	8.0	
parch	0	1.0	0.38	0.81	0.0	0.0	0.0	6.0	
fare	0	1.0	32.2	49.69	0.0	7.91	31.0	512.33	

```
─────────────────── End ───────────────────
```

FIGURE 5.19 An analysis of the Titanic dataset.

WORKING WITH SEABORN

Seaborn is a Python library for data visualization that also provides a high-level interface to Matplotlib. Seaborn is easier to work with than Matplotlib, and actually extends `Matplotlib`, but keep in mind that `Seaborn` is not as powerful as `Matplotlib`.

`Seaborn` addresses two challenges of `Matplotlib`. The first involves the default `Matplotlib` parameters. `Seaborn` works with different parameters, which provides greater flexibility than the default rendering of `Matplotlib` plots. `Seaborn` addresses the limitations of the `Matplotlib` default values for features such as colors, tick marks on the upper and right axes, and the style (among others).

In addition, `Seaborn` makes it easier to plot entire data frames (somewhat like `Pandas`) than doing so in `Matplotlib`. Nevertheless, since `Seaborn` extends `Matplotlib`, knowledge of the latter (discussed in Chapter 6) is advantageous and will simplify your learning curve.

Features of Seaborn

`Seaborn` provides a nice set of features and useful methods to control the display of data, some of which are listed here:

- scale Seaborn plots
- set the plot style
- set the figure size
- rotate label text
- set xlim or ylim
- set log scale
- add titles

Some useful Seaborn methods are listed here:

- `plt.xlabel()`
- `plt.ylabel()`
- `plt.annotate()`
- `plt.legend()`
- `plt.ylim()`
- `plt.savefig()`

`Seaborn` supports various built-in datasets, just like `NumPy` and `Pandas`, including the `Iris` dataset and the `Titanic` dataset, both of which you will see in subsequent sections. As a starting point, the next section contains the code that displays all the available built-in datasets in Seaborn.

SEABORN DATASET NAMES

Listing 5.30 displays the contents `dataset_names.py` that displays the `Seaborn` built-in datasets, one of which we will use in a subsequent section in order to render a heat map in `Seaborn`.

Listing 5.30: dataset_names.py

```
import seaborn as sns

names = sns.get_dataset_names()
for name in names:
  print("name:",name)
```

Listing 5.30 contains an `import` statement, followed by initializing the variable `names` with a list of the dataset names in `Seaborn`. Then a simple loop iterates through the values in the `names` variable and prints their values. The output from Listing 5.30 is here:

```
name: anagrams
name: anscombe
name: attention
name: brain_networks
name: car_crashes
name: diamonds
name: dots
name: exercise
name: flights
name: fmri
name: gammas
name: geyser
name: iris
name: mpg
name: penguins
name: planets
name: taxis
name: tips
```

```
name: titanic
```

The three-line code sample in the next section shows you how to display the rows in the built-in "tips" dataset.

SEABORN BUILT-IN DATASETS

Listing 5.31 displays the contents of `seaborn_tips.py` that illustrates how to read the `tips` dataset into a data frame and display the first five rows of the dataset.

Listing 5.31: seaborn_tips.py

```
import seaborn as sns

df = sns.load_dataset("tips")
print(df.head())
```

Listing 5.31 is very simple: after importing Seaborn, the variable `df` is initialized with the data in the built-in dataset `tips`, and the `print()` statement displays the first five rows of `df`. Note that the `load_dataset()` API searches for online or built-in datasets. The output from Listing 5.31 is here:

	total_bill	tip	sex	smoker	day	time	size
0	16.99	1.01	Female	No	Sun	Dinner	2
1	10.34	1.66	Male	No	Sun	Dinner	3
2	21.01	3.50	Male	No	Sun	Dinner	3
3	23.68	3.31	Male	No	Sun	Dinner	2
4	24.59	3.61	Female	No	Sun	Dinner	4

THE IRIS DATASET IN SEABORN

Listing 5.32 displays the contents of `seaborn_iris.py` that illustrates how to plot the `Iris` dataset.

Listing 5.32: seaborn_iris.py

```
import seaborn as sns
```

```
import matplotlib.pyplot as plt

# Load iris data
iris1 = sns.load_dataset("iris")

# Construct iris plot
sns.swarmplot(x="species", y="petal_length",
data=iris1)

# Show plot
plt.show()
```

Listing 5.32 imports `seaborn` and `Matplotlib.pyplot` and then initializes the variable `iris1` with the contents of the built-in `Iris` dataset. Next, the `swarmplot()` API displays a graph with the horizontal axis labeled `species`, the vertical axis labeled `petal_length`, and the displayed points are from the `Iris` dataset.

Figure 5.20 displays the images in the `Iris` dataset based on the code in Listing 5.32.

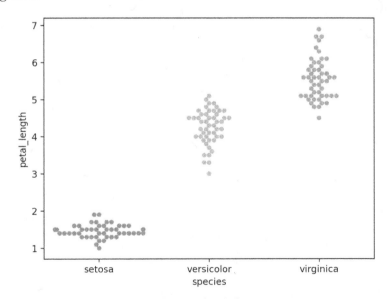

FIGURE 5.20 The Iris dataset.

THE TITANIC DATASET IN SEABORN

Listing 5.33 displays the contents of `seaborn_titanic_plot.py` that illustrates how to plot the `Titanic` dataset.

Listing 5.33: seaborn_titanic_plot.py

```
import matplotlib.pyplot as plt
import seaborn as sns

titanic = sns.load_dataset("titanic")
g = sns.factorplot("class", "survived", "sex",
data=titanic, kind="bar", palette="muted",
legend=False)

plt.show()
```

Listing 5.33 contains the same `import` statements as Listing 5.33, and then initializes the variable `titanic` with the contents of the built-in `Titanic` dataset. Next, the `factorplot()` API displays a graph with dataset attributes that are listed in the API invocation.

Figure 5.21 displays a plot of the data in the `Titanic` dataset based on the code in Listing 5.33.

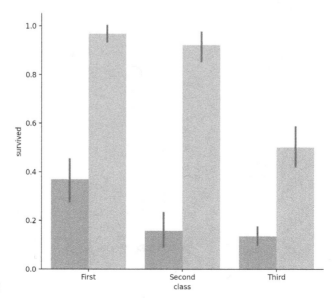

FIGURE 5.21: A HISTOGRAM OF THE TITANIC DATASET.

EXTRACTING DATA FROM TITANIC DATASET IN SEABORN

Listing 5.34 displays the contents of `seaborn_titanic.py` that illustrates how to extract subsets of data from the `Titanic` dataset.

Listing 5.34: seaborn_titanic.py

```
import matplotlib.pyplot as plt
import seaborn as sns

titanic = sns.load_dataset("titanic")
print("titanic info:")
titanic.info()

print("first five rows of titanic:")
print(titanic.head())

print("first four ages:")
print(titanic.loc[0:3,'age'])

print("fifth passenger:")
print(titanic.iloc[4])

#print("first five ages:")
#print(titanic['age'].head())

#print("first five ages and gender:")
#print(titanic[['age','sex']].head())

#print("descending ages:")
#print(titanic.sort_values('age', ascending = False).
head())

#print("older than 50:")
#print(titanic[titanic['age'] > 50])
```

```
#print("embarked (unique):")
#print(titanic['embarked'].unique())

#print("survivor counts:")
#print(titanic['survived'].value_counts())

#print("counts per class:")
#print(titanic['pclass'].value_counts())

#print("max/min/mean/median ages:")
#print(titanic['age'].max())
#print(titanic['age'].min())
#print(titanic['age'].mean())
#print(titanic['age'].median())
```

Listing 5.34 contains the same `import` statements as Listing 5.34, and then initializes the variable `titanic` with the contents of the built-in `Titanic` dataset. The next portion of Listing 5.34 displays various aspects of the `Titanic` dataset, such as its structure, the first five rows, the first four ages, and the details of the fifth passenger.

As you can see, there is a large block of "commented out" code that you can uncomment in order to see the associated output, such as age, gender, persons over 50, unique rows, and so forth. The output from Listing 5.34 is here:

```
titanic info:
<class 'pandas.core.frame.DataFrame'>
RangeIndex: 891 entries, 0 to 890
Data columns (total 15 columns):
survived      891 non-null int64
pclass        891 non-null int64
sex           891 non-null object
age           714 non-null float64
sibsp         891 non-null int64
parch         891 non-null int64
fare          891 non-null float64
```

```
embarked       889 non-null object
class          891 non-null category
who            891 non-null object
adult_male     891 non-null bool
deck           203 non-null category
embark_town    889 non-null object
alive          891 non-null object
alone          891 non-null bool
dtypes: bool(2), category(2), float64(2), int64(4),
object(5)
memory usage: 80.6+ KB
first five rows of titanic:
   survived  pclass     sex   age  sibsp  parch      fare embarked  class  \
0         0       3    male  22.0      1      0    7.2500        S  Third
1         1       1  female  38.0      1      0   71.2833        C  First
2         1       3  female  26.0      0      0    7.9250        S  Third
3         1       1  female  35.0      1      0   53.1000        S  First
4         0       3    male  35.0      0      0    8.0500        S  Third


     who  adult_male deck  embark_town alive  alone
0    man        True  NaN  Southampton    no  False
1  woman       False    C    Cherbourg   yes  False
2  woman       False  NaN  Southampton   yes   True
3  woman       False    C  Southampton   yes  False
4    man        True  NaN  Southampton    no   True
first four ages:
0    22.0
1    38.0
2    26.0
3    35.0
Name: age, dtype: float64
fifth passenger:
survived                 0
pclass                   3
```

```
sex                         male
age                           35
sibsp                          0
parch                          0
fare                        8.05
embarked                       S
class                      Third
who                          man
adult_male                  True
deck                         NaN
embark_town         Southampton
alive                         no
alone                       True
Name: 4, dtype: object
counts per class:
3     491
1     216
2     184
Name: pclass, dtype: int64
max/min/mean/median ages:
80.0
0.42
29.69911764705882
28.0
```

VISUALIZING A PANDAS DATAFRAME IN SEABORN

Listing 5.35 displays the contents of `pandas_seaborn.py` that illustrates how to display a `Pandas` dataset in `Seaborn`.

Listing 5.35: pandas_seaborn.py

```
import pandas as pd
import random
import matplotlib.pyplot as plt
import seaborn as sns
```

```
df = pd.DataFrame()

df['x'] = random.sample(range(1, 100), 25)
df['y'] = random.sample(range(1, 100), 25)

print("top five elements:")
print(df.head())

# display a density plot
#sns.kdeplot(df.y)

# display a density plot
#sns.kdeplot(df.y, df.x)

#sns.distplot(df.x)

# display a histogram
#plt.hist(df.x, alpha=.3)
#sns.rugplot(df.x)

# display a boxplot
#sns.boxplot([df.y, df.x])

# display a violin plot
#sns.violinplot([df.y, df.x])

# display a heatmap
#sns.heatmap([df.y, df.x], annot=True, fmt="d")

# display a cluster map
#sns.clustermap(df)

# display a scatterplot of the data points
sns.lmplot('x', 'y', data=df, fit_reg=False)
plt.show()
```

Listing 5.35 contains several familiar `import` statements, followed by the initialization of the `Pandas` variable `df` as a `Pandas` DataFrame. The next two code snippets initialize the columns and rows of the data frame and the `print()` statement display the first five rows.

For your convenience, Listing 5.35 contains an assortment of "commented out" code snippets that use Seaborn in order to render a density plot, a histogram, a boxplot, a violin plot, a heatmap, and a cluster. Uncomment the portions that interest you in order to see the associated plot. The output from Listing 5.35 is here:

```
top five elements:
     x    y
0   52   34
1   31   47
2   23   18
3   34   70
4   71    1
```

Figure 5.22 displays a plot of the data in the `Titanic` dataset based on the code in Listing 5.35.

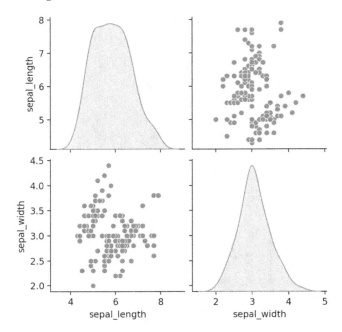

FIGURE 5.22 A Pandas Dataframe displayed via Seaborn.

SEABORN HEAT MAPS

Listing 5.36 displays the contents `sns_heatmap1.py` that displays a heat map from a `Seaborn` built-in dataset.

Listing 5.36: sns_heatmap1.py

```
import seaborn as sns
import matplotlib.pyplot as plt

data = sns.load_dataset("flights")
data = data.pivot("month", "year", "passengers")

print("data.head():")
print(data.head())

sns.heatmap(data)
plt.show()
```

Listing 5.36 contains `import` statements and then initializes the variable `data` with the built-in `flights` dataset. The next code snippet invokes the `pivot()` method that "inverts" the row and columns of the dataset. The final code portion of Listing 5.36 displays the first five rows of the dataset and then generates a heat map based on the dataset. The output from Listing 5.37 is here:

```
data.head():
year    1949  1950  1951  1952  1953  1954  1955  1956
        1957  1958  1959  1960
month
Jan      112   115   145   171   196   204   242   284
         315   340   360   417
Feb      118   126   150   180   196   188   233   277
         301   318   342   391
Mar      132   141   178   193   236   235   267   317
         356   362   406   419
Apr      129   135   163   181   235   227   269   313
         348   348   396   461
May      121   125   172   183   229   234   270   318
         355   363   420   472
```

Figure 5.23 displays a plot of the data in the `Titanic` dataset based on the code in Listing 5.36.

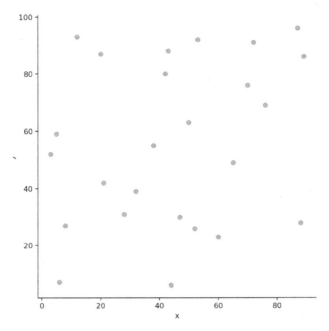

FIGURE 5.23 A Pandas DataFrame displayed via Seaborn.

SEABORN PAIR PLOTS

This section contains several `Python`-based code samples that show you how to use the `Seaborn pair_plot()` method to render pair plots.

Listing 5.37 displays the contents `seaborn_pairplot1.py` that displays a pair plot with the `Iris` dataset.

Listing 5.37: seaborn_pairplot1.py

```
import seaborn as sns
import pandas as pd
import matplotlib.pyplot as plt
```

```
# load iris data
iris = sns.load_dataset("iris")

df = pd.DataFrame(iris)

# construct and display iris plot
g = sns.pairplot(df, height=2, aspect=1.0)
plt.show()
```

Listing 5.38 contains `import` statements and then initializes the variable `iris` with the built-in `Iris` dataset. The next code snippet initializes the DataFrame `df` with the contents of the `Iris` dataset. The final code portion of Listing 5.38 constructs a pair plot of the `Iris` dataset and then displays the output. Figure 5.24 displays a plot of the data in the `Titanic` dataset based on the code in Listing 5.38.

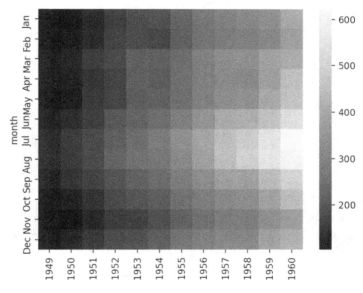

FIGURE 5.24 A Seaborn pair plot.

Listing 5.39 displays the contents `seaborn_pairplot2.py` that displays a pair plot with the `Iris` dataset.

Listing 5.39: seaborn_pairplot2.py

```python
import seaborn as sns
import pandas as pd
import matplotlib.pyplot as plt

# load iris data
iris = sns.load_dataset("iris")

df = pd.DataFrame(iris)

# IRIS columns:
# sepal_length,sepal_width,petal_length,petal_
width,species

# plot a subset of columns:
plot_columns = ['sepal_length', 'sepal_width']
sns.pairplot(df[plot_columns])
plt.show()

# specify KDE for the diagonal:
sns.pairplot(df[plot_columns], diag_kind='kde')
plt.show()
```

Listing 5.39 is similar to the code in Listing 5.38: the difference is that the former selects only two features in the `Iris` dataset instead of all the features in the `Iris` dataset.

The next code portion of Listing 5.39 constructs a pair plot of the `Iris` dataset and then displays the output, followed by another pair plot that specifies the `kde` value for the `diag_kind` parameter. The acronym ode refers to "kernel density estimation," which is discussed in the Seaborn documentation here:

https://seaborn.pydata.org/tutorial/distributions.html#tutorial-kde

Launch the code in Listing 5.39 and you will see a pair plot displayed as shown in Figure 5.25.

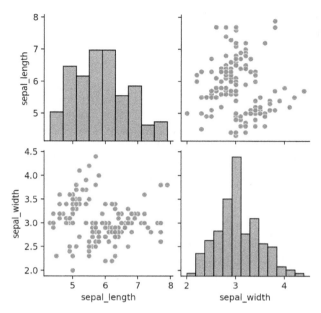

FIGURE 5.25 A Seaborn pair plot.

Figure 5.26 displays a plot of the data with the `kde` option for the `Iris` dataset based on the code in Listing 5.39.

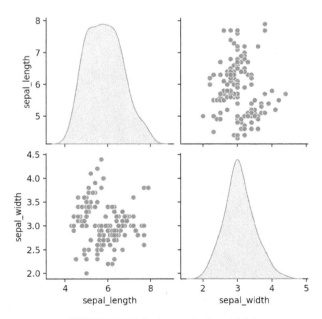

FIGURE 5.26 A Seaborn pair plot with kde.

SUMMARY

This chapter started with a very short introduction to data visualization and `Matplotlib`, along with code samples that displayed the available styles in colors in `Matplotlib`.

Then you learned how to render horizontal lines, slanted lines, parallel lines, and a grid of points. In addition, you learned how to load images, display checkerboard patterns, and plot trigonometric functions. Moreover, you saw how to render histograms, bar charts, pie charts, heat maps.

Finally, you learned how to render charts and graphs using the Seaborn open-source library.

INTRODUCTION TO PYTHON

This appendix contains an introduction to Python, with information about useful tools for installing Python modules, basic Python constructs, and how to work with some data types in Python.

The first part of this appendix covers how to install Python, some Python environment variables, and how to use the Python interpreter. You will see Python code samples and also how to save Python code in text files that you can launch from the command line. The second part of this appendix shows you how to work with simple data types, such as numbers, fractions, and strings. The final part of this appendix discusses exceptions and how to use them in Python scripts.

Note: the Python code samples in this book are for Python 3.x.

TOOLS FOR PYTHON

The Anaconda Python distribution is available for Windows, Linux, and Mac, and it's downloadable here:

http://continuum.io/downloads

Anaconda is well-suited for modules such as NumPy and scipy (not discussed in this book), and if you are a Windows user, Anaconda appears to be a better alternative.

easy_install and pip

Both easy_install and pip are very easy to use when you need to install Python modules.

Whenever you need to install a `Python` module (and there are many in this book), use either `easy_install` or `pip` with the following syntax:

```
easy_install <module-name>
pip install <module-name>
```

Note: `Python`-based modules are easier to install, whereas modules with code written in C are usually faster but more difficult in terms of installation.

virtualenv

The `virtualenv` tool enables you to create isolated Python environments, and its home page is here:

http://www.virtualenv.org/en/latest/virtualenv.html

`virtualenv` addresses the problem of preserving the correct dependencies and versions (and indirectly permissions) for different applications. If you are a `Python` novice you might not need `virtualenv` right now, but keep this tool in mind.

IPython

Another very good tool is `IPython` (which won a Jolt award), and its home page is here:

http://ipython.org/install.html

Type `ipython` to invoke IPython from the command line:

```
ipython
```

The preceding command displays the following output:

```
Python 3.9.13 (main, May 24 2022, 21:28:12)
Type 'copyright', 'credits' or 'license' for more
information
IPython 8.14.0 -- An enhanced Interactive Python.
Type '?' for help.

In [1]:
```

Next type a question mark ("?") at the prompt and you will see some useful information, a portion of which is here:

```
IPython -- An enhanced Interactive Python
==========================================


IPython offers a fully compatible replacement for the
standard Python
interpreter, with convenient shell features, special
commands, command
history mechanism and output results caching.


At your system command line, type 'ipython -h' to see
the command line
options available. This document only describes
interactive features.


GETTING HELP
------------


Within IPython you have various way to access help:

    ?          -> Introduction and overview of IPython's
    features (this screen).
    object?    -> Details about 'object'.
    object??   -> More detailed, verbose information about
    'object'.
    %quickref -> Quick reference of all IPython specific
    syntax and magics.
    help       -> Access Python's own help system.


If you are in terminal IPython you can quit this screen
by pressing `q`.
```

Finally, simply type `quit` at the command prompt and you will exit the ipython shell.

The next section shows you how to check whether or not `Python` is installed on your machine, and also where you can download `Python`.

PYTHON INSTALLATION

Before you download anything, check if you have `Python` already installed on your machine (which is likely if you have a Macbook or a Linux machine) by typing the following command in a command shell:

```
python -V
```

The output for the Macbook used in this book is here:

```
python 3.9.1
```

Note: install Python 3.9 (or as close as possible to this version) on your machine so that you will have the same version of `Python` that was used to test the `Python` scripts in this book.

If you need to install `Python` on your machine, navigate to this website:

http://www.python.org/download

In addition, `PythonWin` is available for Windows, and its home page is here:

http://www.cgl.ucsf.edu/Outreach/pc204/pythonwin.html

Use any text editor that can create, edit, and save `Python` scripts and save them as plain text files (don't use Microsoft Word).

After you have `Python` installed and configured on your machine, you are ready to work with the `Python` scripts in this book.

SETTING THE `PATH` ENVIRONMENT VARIABLE (WINDOWS ONLY)

The `PATH` environment variable specifies a list of directories that are searched whenever you specify an executable program from the command line. A very good guide to setting up your environment so that the `Python` executable is always available in every command shell is to follow the instructions here:

http://www.blog.pythonlibrary.org/2011/11/24/python-101-setting-up-python-on-windows/

LAUNCHING PYTHON ON YOUR MACHINE

There are three different ways to launch `Python`:

- Use the `Python` Interactive Interpreter.
- Launch `Python` scripts from the command line.
- Use an IDE.

The next section shows you how to launch the `Python` interpreter from the command line, and later in this appendix you will learn how to launch Python scripts from the command line and also about `Python` IDEs.

Note: the emphasis in this book is to launch `Python` scripts from the command line or to enter code in the Python interpreter.

The Python Interactive Interpreter

Launch the `Python` interactive interpreter from the command line by opening a command shell and typing the following command:

```
python
```

You will see the following prompt (or something similar):

```
Python 3.9.1 (v3.9.1:1e5d33e9b9, Dec  7 2020, 12:44:01)
[Clang 12.0.0 (clang-1200.0.32.27)] on darwin
Type "help", "copyright", "credits" or "license" for
more information.
>>>
```

Now type the expression `2 + 7` at the prompt:

```
>>> 2 + 7
Python displays the following result:
9
>>>
```

Type `quit()` to exit the `Python` shell.

You can launch any `Python` script from the command line by preceding it with the word "python." For example, if you have a `Python` script `myscript.py` that contains Python commands, launch the script as follows:

```
python myscript.py
```

As a simple illustration, suppose that the Python script `myscript.py` contains the following Python code:

```
print('Hello World from Python')
print('2 + 7 = ', 2+7)
```

When you launch the preceding Python script you will see the following output:

```
Hello World from Python
2 + 7 =  9
```

PYTHON IDENTIFIERS

A Python identifier is the name of a variable, function, class, module, or other Python object, and a valid identifier conforms to the following rules:

* It starts with a letter A to Z, or a to z, or an underscore (_).
* It contains zero or more letters, underscores, and digits (0 to 9).

Note: Python identifiers cannot contain characters such as @, $, and %. Python is a case-sensitive language, so Abc and abc are different identifiers in Python.

In addition, Python has the following naming convention:

* Class names start with an uppercase letter and all other identifiers with a lowercase letter.
* An initial underscore is used for private identifiers.
* Two initial underscores are used for strongly private identifiers.

A Python identifier with two initial underscore and two trailing underscore characters indicates a language-defined special name.

LINES, INDENTATION, AND MULTILINES

Unlike other programming languages (such as Java or Objective-C), Python uses indentation instead of curly braces for code blocks. Indentation must be consistent in a code block, as shown here:

```
if True:
    print("ABC")
```

```
        print("DEF")
else:
        print("ABC")
        print("DEF")
```

Multiline statements in `Python` can terminate with a new line or the backslash ("\") character, as shown here:

```
total = x1 + \
        x2 + \
        x3
```

Obviously you can place x1, x2, and x3 on the same line, so there is no reason to use three separate lines; however, this functionality is available in case you need to add a set of variables that do not fit on a single line.

You can specify multiple statements in one line by using a semicolon (";") to separate each statement, as shown here:

```
a=10; b=5; print(a); print(a+b)
```

The output of the preceding code snippet is here:

```
10
15
```

Note: the use of semi-colons and the continuation character are discouraged in Python.

QUOTATION AND COMMENTS IN PYTHON

`Python` allows single ('), double (") and triple (''' or """) quotes for string literals, provided that they match at the beginning and the end of the string. You can use triple quotes for strings that span multiple lines. The following examples are legal Python strings:

```
word = 'word'
line = "This is a sentence."
para = """This is a paragraph. This paragraph contains
more than one sentence."""
```

A string literal that begins with the letter "r" (for "raw") treats everything as a literal character and "escapes" the meaning of meta characters, as shown here:

```
a1 = r'\n'
a2 = r'\r'
a3 = r'\t'
print('a1:',a1,'a2:',a2,'a3:',a3)
```

The output of the preceding code block is here:

```
a1: \n a2: \r a3: \t
```

You can embed a single quote in a pair of double quotes (and vice versa) in order to display a single quote or a double quote. Another way to accomplish the same result is to precede a single or double quote with a backslash ("\") character. The following code block illustrates these techniques:

```
b1 = "'"
b2 = '"'
b3 = '\''
b4 = "\""
print('b1:',b1,'b2:',b2)
print('b3:',b3,'b4:',b4)
```

The output of the preceding code block is here:

```
b1: ' b2: "
b3: ' b4: "
```

A hash sign (#) that is not inside a string literal is the character that indicates the beginning of a comment. Moreover, all characters after the # and up to the physical line end are part of the comment (and ignored by the Python interpreter). Consider the following code block:

```
#!/usr/bin/python
# First comment
print("Hello, Python!")  # second comment
```

This will produce following result:

```
Hello, Python!
```

A comment may be on the same line after a statement or expression:

```
name = "Tom Jones" # This is also comment
```

You can comment multiple lines as follows:

```
# This is comment one
# This is comment two
# This is comment three
```

A blank line in Python is a line containing only whitespace, a comment, or both.

SAVING YOUR CODE IN A MODULE

Earlier you saw how to launch the `Python` interpreter from the command line and then enter `Python` commands. However, that everything that you type in the `Python` interpreter is only valid for the current session: if you exit the interpreter and then launch the interpreter again, your previous definitions are no longer valid. Fortunately, `Python` enables you to store code in a text file, as discussed in the next section.

A *module* in `Python` is a text file that contains `Python` statements. In the previous section, you saw how the `Python` interpreter enables you to test code snippets whose definitions are valid for the current session. If you want to retain the code snippets and other definitions, place them in a text file so that you can execute that code outside of the Python interpreter.

The outermost statements in a `Python` are executed from top to bottom when the module is imported for the first time, which will then set up its variables and functions.

A `Python` module can be run directly from the command line, as shown here:

```
python First.py
```

As an illustration, place the following two statements in a text file called `First.py`:

```
x = 3
print(x)
```

Now type the following command:

```
python First.py
```

The output from the preceding command is 3, which is the same as executing the preceding code from the `Python` interpreter.

When a `Python` module is run directly, the special variable `__name__` is set to `__main__`. You will often see the following type of code in a `Python` module:

```
if __name__ == '__main__':
    # do something here
    print('Running directly')
```

The preceding code snippet enables `Python` to determine if a `Python` module was launched from the command line or imported into another `Python` module.

SOME STANDARD MODULES IN PYTHON

The `Python` Standard Library provides many modules that can simplify your own `Python` scripts. A list of the Standard Library modules is here:

http://www.python.org/doc

Some of the most important `Python` modules include `cgi`, `math`, `os`, `pickle`, `random`, `re`, `socket`, `sys`, `time`, and `urllib`.

The code samples in this book use the modules `math`, `os`, `random`, `re`, `socket`, `sys`, `time`, and `urllib`. You need to import these modules in order to use them in your code. For example, the following code block shows you how to import four standard `Python` modules:

```
import datetime
import re
import sys
import time
```

The code samples in this book import one or more of the preceding modules, as well as other Python modules.

THE `HELP()` AND `DIR()` FUNCTIONS

An Internet search for `Python`-related topics usually returns a number of links with useful information. Alternatively, you can check the official `Python` documentation site: *docs.python.org*

In addition, `Python` provides the `help()` and `dir()` functions that are accessible from the `Python` interpreter. The `help()` function displays documentation strings, whereas the `dir()` function displays defined symbols.

For example, if you type `help(sys)` you will see documentation for the `sys` module, whereas `dir(sys)` displays a list of the defined symbols.

Type the following command in the `Python` interpreter to display the string-related methods in `Python`:

```
>>> dir(str)
```

The preceding command generates the following output:

```
['__add__', '__class__', '__contains__', '__delattr__',
'__doc__', '__eq__', '__format__', '__ge__', '__
getattribute__', '__getitem__', '__getnewargs__',
'__getslice__', '__gt__', '__hash__', '__init__',
'__le__', '__len__', '__lt__', '__mod__', '__mul__',
'__ne__', '__new__', '__reduce__', '__reduce_ex__',
'__repr__', '__rmod__', '__rmul__', '__setattr__',
'__sizeof__', '__str__', '__subclasshook__', '_
formatter_field_name_split', '_formatter_parser',
'capitalize', 'center', 'count', 'decode', 'encode',
'endswith', 'expandtabs', 'find', 'format', 'index',
'isalnum', 'isalpha', 'isdigit', 'islower', 'isspace',
'istitle', 'isupper', 'join', 'ljust', 'lower',
'lstrip', 'partition', 'replace', 'rfind', 'rindex',
'rjust', 'rpartition', 'rsplit', 'rstrip', 'split',
'splitlines', 'startswith', 'strip', 'swapcase',
'title', 'translate', 'upper', 'zfill']
```

The preceding list gives you a consolidated "dump" of built-in functions (including some that are discussed later in this appendix). Although the `max()` function obviously returns the maximum value of its arguments, the purpose of other functions such as `filter()` or `map()` is not immediately apparent (unless you have used them in other programming languages). In any case, the preceding list provides a starting point for finding out more about various Python built-in functions that are not discussed in this appendix.

Note that while `dir()` does not list the names of built-in functions and variables, you can obtain this information from the standard module __builtin__ that is automatically imported under the name __builtins__:

```
>>> dir(__builtins__)
```

The following command shows you how to get more information about a function:

```
help(str.lower)
```

The output from the preceding command is here:

```
Help on method_descriptor:

lower(...)
    S.lower() -> string

    Return a copy of the string S converted to
    lowercase.
(END)
```

Check the online documentation and also experiment with `help()` and `dir()` when you need additional information about a particular function or module.

COMPILE TIME AND RUNTIME CODE CHECKING

`Python` performs some compile-time checking, but most checks (including type, name, and so forth) are *deferred* until code execution. Consequently, if your `Python` code references a user-defined function that that does not exist, the code will compile successfully. In fact, the code will fail with an exception *only* when the code execution path references the nonexistent function.

As a simple example, consider the following `Python` function `myFunc` that references the nonexistent function called `DoesNotExist`:

```
def myFunc(x):
    if x == 3:
        print(DoesNotExist(x))
    else:
        print('x: ',x)
```

The preceding code will only fail when the `myFunc` function is passed the value 3, after which `Python` raises an error.

Now that you understand some basic concepts (such as how to use the `Python` interpreter) and how to launch your custom `Python` modules, the next section discusses primitive data types in Python.

SIMPLE DATA TYPES IN PYTHON

`Python` supports primitive data types, such as numbers (integers, floating point numbers, and exponential numbers), strings, and dates. `Python` also supports more complex data types, such as lists (or arrays), tuples, and dictionaries. The next several sections discuss some of the `Python` primitive data types, along with code snippets that show you how to perform various operations on those data types.

WORKING WITH NUMBERS

`Python` provides arithmetic operations for manipulating numbers a straightforward manner that is similar to other programming languages. The following examples involve arithmetic operations on integers:

```
>>> 2+2
4
>>> 4/3
1
>>> 3*8
24
```

The following example assigns numbers to two variables and computes their product:

```
>>> x = 4
>>> y = 7
>>> x * y
28
```

The following examples demonstrate arithmetic operations involving integers:

```
>>> 2+2
```

```
4
>>> 4/3
1
>>> 3*8
24
```

Notice that division ("/") of two integers is actually truncation in which only the integer result is retained. The following example converts a floating point number into exponential form:

```
>>> fnum = 0.00012345689000007
>>> "%.14e"%fnum
'1.23456890000070e-04'
```

You can use the `int()` function and the `float()` function to convert strings to numbers:

```
word1 = "123"
word2 = "456.78"
var1 = int(word1)
var2 = float(word2)
print("var1: ",var1," var2: ",var2)
```

The output from the preceding code block is here:

```
var1:  123  var2:  456.78
```

Alternatively, you can use the `eval()` function:

```
word1 = "123"
word2 = "456.78"
var1 = eval(word1)
var2 = eval(word2)
print("var1: ",var1," var2: ",var2)
```

If you attempt to convert a string that is not a valid integer or a floating point number, Python raises an exception, so it's advisable to place your code in a `try/except` block (discussed later in this appendix).

Working With Other Bases

Numbers in Python are in base 10 (the default), but you can easily convert numbers to other bases. For example, the following code block initializes the variable x with the value `1234`, and then displays that number in base `2`, `8`, and `16`, respectively:

```
>>> x = 1234
>>> bin(x) '0b10011010010'
>>> oct(x) '0o2322'
>>> hex(x) '0x4d2'
```

Use the `format()` function if you wan to suppress the `0b`, `0o`, or `0x` prefixes, as shown here:

```
>>> format(x, 'b') '10011010010'
>>> format(x, 'o') '2322'
>>> format(x, 'x') '4d2'
```

Negative integers are displayed with a negative sign:

```
>>> x = -1234
>>> format(x, 'b') '-10011010010'
>>> format(x, 'x') '-4d2'
```

The `chr()` Function

The `Python` `chr()` function takes a positive integer as a parameter and converts it to its corresponding alphabetic value (if one exists). The letters A through Z have decimal representation of `65` through `91` (which corresponds to hexadecimal `41` through `5b`), and the lowercase letters a through z have decimal representation `97` through `122` (hexadecimal `61` through `7b`).

Here is an example of using the `chr()` function to print uppercase A:

```
>>> x=chr(65)
>>> x
'A'
```

The following code block prints the ASCII values for a range of integers:

```
result = ""
for x in range(65,91):
  print(x, chr(x))
  result = result+chr(x)+' '
print("result: ",result)
```

Note: `Python` 2 uses ASCII strings whereas `Python` 3 uses UTF-8.

You can represent a range of characters with the following line:

```
for x in range(65,91):
```

However, the following equivalent code snippet is more intuitive:

```
for x in range(ord('A'), ord('Z')):
```

If you want to display the result for lowercase letters, change the preceding range from `(65,91)` to either of the following statements:

```
for x in range(65,91):
for x in range(ord('a'), ord('z')):
```

The round() Function in Python

The `Python round()` function enables you to round decimal values to the nearest precision:

```
>>> round(1.23, 1)
1.2
>>> round(-3.42,1)
-3.4
```

Formatting Numbers in Python

`Python` allows you to specify the number of decimal places of precision to use when printing decimal numbers, as shown here:

```
>>> x = 1.23456
>>> format(x, '0.2f')
'1.23'
>>> format(x, '0.3f')
'1.235'
>>> 'value is {:0.3f}'.format(x) 'value is 1.235'
>>> from decimal import Decimal
>>> a = Decimal('4.2')
>>> b = Decimal('2.1')
>>> a + b
Decimal('6.3')
>>> print(a + b)
6.3
```

```
>>> (a + b) == Decimal('6.3')
True
>>> x = 1234.56789
>>> # Two decimal places of accuracy
>>> format(x, '0.2f')
'1234.57'
>>> # Right justified in 10 chars, one-digit accuracy
>>> format(x, '>10.1f')
'    1234.6'
>>> # Left justified
>>> format(x, '<10.1f') '1234.6    '
>>> # Centered
>>> format(x, '^10.1f') '  1234.6  '
>>> # Inclusion of thousands separator
>>> format(x, ',')
'1,234.56789'
>>> format(x, '0,.1f')
'1,234.6'
```

WORKING WITH FRACTIONS

Python supports the Fraction() function (which is define in the fractions module) that accepts two integers that represent the numerator and the denominator (which must be nonzero) of a fraction. Several example of defining and manipulating fractions in Python are shown here:

```
>>> from fractions import Fraction
>>> a = Fraction(5, 4)
>>> b = Fraction(7, 16)
>>> print(a + b)
27/16
>>> print(a * b) 35/64
>>> # Getting numerator/denominator
>>> c = a * b
>>> c.numerator
```

```
35
>>> c.denominator 64
>>> # Converting to a float >>> float(c)
0.546875
>>> # Limiting the denominator of a value
>>> print(c.limit_denominator(8))
4
>>> # Converting a float to a fraction >>> x = 3.75
>>> y = Fraction(*x.as_integer_ratio())
>>> y
Fraction(15, 4)
```

Before delving into `Python` code samples that work with strings, the next section briefly discusses `Unicode` and UTF-8, both of which are character encodings.

UNICODE AND UTF-8

A `Unicode` string consists of a sequence of numbers that are between `0` and `0x10ffff`, where each number represents a group of bytes. An encoding is the manner in which a `Unicode` string is translated into a sequence of bytes. Among the various encodings, `UTF-8` ("Unicode Transformation Format") is perhaps the most common, and it's also the default encoding for many systems. The digit 8 in `UTF-8` indicates that the encoding uses 8-bit numbers, whereas `UTF-16` uses 16-bit numbers (but this encoding is less common).

The ASCII character set is a subset of `UTF-8`, so a valid ASCII string can be read as a `UTF-8` string without any re-encoding required. In addition, a Unicode string can be converted into a `UTF-8` string.

WORKING WITH UNICODE

Python supports `Unicode`, which means that you can render characters in different languages. `Unicode` data can be stored and manipulated in the same way as strings. Create a `Unicode` string by prepending the letter "u," as shown here:

```
>>> u'Hello from Python!'
```

```
u'Hello from Python!'
```

Special characters can be included in a string by specifying their `Unicode` value. For example, the following `Unicode` string embeds a space (which has the `Unicode` value 0x0020) in a string:

```
>>> u'Hello\u0020from Python!'
u'Hello from Python!'
```

Listing A.1 displays the contents of `Unicode1.py` that illustrates how to display a string of characters in Japanese and another string of characters in Chinese (Mandarin).

Listing A.1: Unicode1.py

```
chinese1 = u'\u5c07\u63a2\u8a0e HTML5 \u53ca\u5176\
u4ed6'
hiragana = u'D3 \u306F \u304B\u3063\u3053\u3043\u3043 \
u3067\u3059!'

print('Chinese:',chinese1)
print('Hiragana:',hiragana)
```

The output of Listing A.1 is here:

```
Chinese: 將探討 HTML5 及其他
Hiragana: D3 は かっこいい です!
```

The next portion of this appendix shows you how to "slice and dice" text strings with built-in `Python` functions.

WORKING WITH STRINGS

A string in `Python2` is a sequence of ASCII-encoded bytes. You can concatenate two strings using the '+' operator. The following example prints a string and then concatenates two single-letter strings:

```
>>> 'abc'
'abc'
>>> 'a' + 'b'
'ab'
```

You can use '+' or '*' to concatenate identical strings, as shown here:

```
>>> 'a' + 'a' + 'a'
'aaa'
>>> 'a' * 3
'aaa'
```

You can assign strings to variables and print them using the `print()` statement:

```
>>> print('abc')
abc
>>> x = 'abc'
>>> print(x)
abc
>>> y = 'def'
>>> print(x + y)
abcdef
```

You can "unpack" the letters of a string and assign them to variables, as shown here:

```
>>> str = "World"
>>> x1,x2,x3,x4,x5 = str
>>> x1
'W'
>>> x2
'o'
>>> x3
'r'
>>> x4
'l'
>>> x5
'd'
```

The preceding code snippets shows you how easy it is to extract the letters in a text string. You can extract substrings of a string as shown in the following examples:

```
>>> x = "abcdef"
```

```
>>> x[0]
'a'
>>> x[-1]
'f'
>>> x[1:3]
'bc'
>>> x[0:2] + x[5:]
'abf'
```

However, you will cause an error if you attempt to subtract two strings, as you probably expect:

```
>>> 'a' - 'b'
Traceback (most recent call last):
  File "<stdin>", line 1, in <module>
TypeError: unsupported operand type(s) for -: 'str' and
'str'
```

The `try/except` construct in `Python` (discussed later in this appendix) enables you to handle the preceding type of exception more gracefully.

Comparing Strings

You can use the methods `lower()` and `upper()` to convert a string to lowercase and uppercase, respectively, as shown here:

```
>>> 'Python'.lower()
'python'
>>> 'Python'.upper()
'PYTHON'
>>>
```

The methods `lower()` and `upper()` are useful for performing a case insensitive comparison of two ASCII strings. Listing A.2 displays the contents of `Compare.py` that uses the `lower()` function in order to compare two ASCII strings.

Listing A.2: Compare.py

```
x = 'Abc'
y = 'abc'
```

```
if(x == y):
  print('x and y: identical')
elif (x.lower() == y.lower()):
  print('x and y: case insensitive match')
else:
  print('x and y: different')
```

Since x contains mixed case letters and y contains lowercase letters, Listing A.2 displays the following output:

```
x and y: different
```

Formatting Strings in Python

`Python` provides the functions `string.lstring()`, `string.rstring()`, and `string.center()` for positioning a text string so that it is left-justified, right-justified, and centered, respectively. As you saw in a previous section, `Python` also provides the `format()` method for advanced interpolation features.

Now enter the following commands in the `Python` interpreter:

```
import string

str1 = 'this is a string'
print(string.ljust(str1, 10))
print(string.rjust(str1, 40))
print(string.center(str1,40))
```

The output is shown here:

```
this is a string
                        this is a string
            this is a string
```

UNINITIALIZED VARIABLES AND THE VALUE NONE IN PYTHON

`Python` distinguishes between an uninitialized variable and the value `None`. The former is a variable that has not been assigned a value, whereas the value

None is a value that indicates "no value." Collections and methods often return the value None, and you can test for the value None in conditional logic.

The next portion of this appendix shows you how to "slice and dice" text strings with built-in Python functions.

SLICING AND SPLICING STRINGS

Python enables you to extract substrings of a string (called "slicing") using array notation. Slice notation is start:stop:step, where the start, stop, and step values are integers that specify the start value, end value, and the increment value. The interesting part about slicing in Python is that you can use the value -1, which operates from the right-side instead of the left-side of a string.

Some examples of slicing a string are here:

```
text1 = "this is a string"
print('First 7 characters:',text1[0:7])
print('Characters 2-4:',text1[2:4])
print('Right-most character:',text1[-1])
print('Right-most 2 characters:',text1[-3:-1])
```

The output from the preceding code block is here:

```
First 7 characters: this is
Characters 2-4: is
Right-most character: g
Right-most 2 characters: in
```

Later in this appendix you will see how to insert a string in the middle of another string.

Testing for Digits and Alphabetic Characters

Python enables you to examine each character in a string and then test whether that character is a bona fide digit or an alphabetic character. This section provides a simple introduction to regular expressions.

Listing A.3 displays the contents of CharTypes.py that illustrates how to determine if a string contains digits or characters. Although we have not discussed if statements in Python, the examples in Listing A.3 are straight-forward.

Listing A.3: CharTypes.py

```
str1 = "4"
str2 = "4234"
str3 = "b"
str4 = "abc"
str5 = "a1b2c3"

if(str1.isdigit()):
   print("this is a digit:",str1)

if(str2.isdigit()):
   print("this is a digit:",str2)

if(str3.isalpha()):
   print("this is alphabetic:",str3)

if(str4.isalpha()):
   print("this is alphabetic:",str4)

if(not str5.isalpha()):
   print("this is not pure alphabetic:",str5)

print("capitalized first letter:",str5.title())
```

Listing A.3 initializes some variables, followed by 2 conditional tests that check whether or not str1 and str2 are digits using the isdigit() function. The next portion of Listing A.3 checks if str3, str4, and str5 are alphabetic strings using the isalpha() function. The output of Listing A.3 is here:

```
this is a digit: 4
this is a digit: 4234
this is alphabetic: b
this is alphabetic: abc
this is not pure alphabetic: a1b2c3
capitalized first letter: A1B2C3
```

SEARCH AND REPLACE A STRING IN OTHER STRINGS

`Python` provides methods for searching and also for replacing a string in a second text string. Listing A.4 displays the contents of `FindPos1.py` that shows you how to use the find function to search for the occurrence of one string in another string.

Listing A.4: FindPos1.py

```
item1 = 'abc'
item2 = 'Abc'
text = 'This is a text string with abc'

pos1 = text.find(item1)
pos2 = text.find(item2)

print('pos1=',pos1)
print('pos2=',pos2)
```

Listing A.4 initializes the variables `item1`, `item2`, and `text`, and then searches for the index of the contents of `item1` and `item2` in the string text. The `Python` `find()` function returns the column number where the first successful match occurs; otherwise, the `find()` function returns a `-1` if a match is unsuccessful. The output from launching Listing A.4 is here:

```
pos1= 27
pos2= -1
```

In addition to the `find()` method, you can use the `in` operator when you want to test for the presence of an element, as shown here:

```
>>> lst = [1,2,3]
>>> 1 in lst
True
```

Listing A.5 displays the contents of `Replace1.py` that shows you how to replace one string with another string.

Listing A.5: Replace1.py

```
text = 'This is a text string with abc'
```

```
print('text:',text)
text = text.replace('is a', 'was a')
print('text:',text)
```

Listing A.5 starts by initializing the variable text and then printing its contents. The next portion of Listing A.5 replaces the occurrence of "is a" with "was a" in the string text, and then prints the modified string. The output from launching Listing A.5 is here:

```
text: This is a text string with abc
text: This was a text string with abc
```

REMOVE LEADING AND TRAILING CHARACTERS

Python provides the functions strip(), lstrip(), and rstrip() to remove characters in a text string. Listing A.6 displays the contents of Remove1.py that shows you how to search for a string.

Listing A.6 Remove1.py

```
text = '   leading and trailing white space   '
print('text1:','x',text,'y')

text = text.lstrip()
print('text2:','x',text,'y')

text = text.rstrip()
print('text3:','x',text,'y')
```

Listing A.6 starts by concatenating the letter x and the contents of the variable text, and then printing the result. The second part of Listing A.6 removes the leading white spaces in the string text and then appends the result to the letter x. The third part of Listing A.6 removes the trailing white spaces in the string text (note that the leading white spaces have already been removed) and then appends the result to the letter x.

The output from launching Listing A.6 is here:

```
text1: x   leading and trailing white space   y
text2: x leading and trailing white space   y
```

```
text3: x leading and trailing white space y
```

If you want to remove extra white spaces inside a text string, use the `replace()` function as discussed in the previous section. The following example illustrates how this can be accomplished, which also contains the `re` module for regular expressions:

```
import re
text = 'a     b'
a = text.replace(' ', '')
b = re.sub('\s+', ' ', text)


print(a)
print(b)
```

The result is here:

```
ab
a b
```

PRINTING TEXT WITHOUT NEWLINE CHARACTERS

If you need to suppress white space and a newline between objects output with multiple print statements, you can use concatenation or the `write()` function.

The first technique is to concatenate the string representations of each object using the `str()` function prior to printing the result. For example, run the following statement in Python:

```
x = str(9)+str(0xff)+str(-3.1)
print('x: ',x)
```

The output is shown here:

```
x:    9255-3.1
```

The preceding line contains the concatenation of the numbers 9 and 255 (which is the decimal value of the hexadecimal number `0xff`) and `-3.1`.

Incidentally, you can use the `str()` function with modules and user-defined classes. An example involving the Python built-in module `sys` is here:

```
>>> import sys
```

```
>>> print(str(sys))
<module 'sys' (built-in)>
```

The following code snippet illustrates how to use the `write()` function to display a string:

```
import sys
write = sys.stdout.write
write('123')
write('123456789')
```

The output is here:

```
1233
1234567899
```

TEXT ALIGNMENT

```
Python provides the methods ljust(), rjust(), and
center() for aligning text. The ljust() and rjust()
functions left justify and right justify a text string,
respectively, whereas the center() function will center
a string. An example is shown in the following code
block:
text = 'Hello World'
text.ljust(20)
'Hello World '
>>> text.rjust(20)
' Hello World'
>>> text.center(20)
' Hello World '
```

You can use the `Python format()` function to align text. Use the `<`, `>`, or `^` characters, along with a desired width, in order to right justify, left justify, and center the text, respectively. The following examples illustrate how you can specify text justification:

```
>>> format(text, '>20')
'         Hello World'
>>>
```

```
>>> format(text, '<20')
'Hello World         '
>>>
>>> format(text, '^20')
'    Hello World     '
>>>
```

WORKING WITH DATES

`Python` provides a rich set of date-related functions that are documented here:

http://docs.python.org/2/library/datetime.html

Listing A.7 displays the contents of the `Python` script `Datetime2.py` that displays various date-related values, such as the current date and time; the day of the week, month, and year; and the time in seconds since the epoch.

Listing A.7: Datetime2.py

```
import time
import datetime

print("Time in seconds since the epoch: %s" %time.
time())
print("Current date and time: " , datetime.datetime.
now())
print("Or like this: " ,datetime.datetime.now().
strftime("%y-%m-%d-%H-%M"))

print("Current year: ", datetime.date.today().
strftime("%Y"))
print("Month of year: ", datetime.date.today().
strftime("%B"))
print("Week number of the year: ", datetime.date.
today().strftime("%W"))
print("Weekday of the week: ", datetime.date.today().
strftime("%w"))
```

```
print("Day of year: ", datetime.date.today().
strftime("%j"))
print("Day of the month : ", datetime.date.today().
strftime("%d"))
print("Day of week: ", datetime.date.today().
strftime("%A"))
```

Listing A.8 displays the output generated by running the code in Listing A.7.

Listing A.8: datetime2.out

```
Time in seconds since the epoch: 1375144195.66
Current date and time:  2013-07-29 17:29:55.664164
Or like this:  13-07-29-17-29
Current year:  2013
Month of year:  July
Week number of the year:  30
Weekday of the week:  1
Day of year:  210
Day of the month :  29
Day of week:  Monday
```

Python also enables you to perform arithmetic calculates with date-related values, as shown in the following code block:

```
>>> from datetime import timedelta
>>> a = timedelta(days=2, hours=6)
>>> b = timedelta(hours=4.5)
>>> c = a + b
>>> c.days
2
>>> c.seconds
37800
>>> c.seconds / 3600
10.5
>>> c.total_seconds() / 3600
58.5
```

Converting Strings to Dates

Listing A.9 displays the contents of `String2Date.py` that illustrates how to convert a string to a date, and also how to calculate the difference between two dates.

Listing A.9: String2Date.py

```
from datetime import datetime

text = '2014-08-13'
y = datetime.strptime(text, '%Y-%m-%d')
z = datetime.now()
diff = z - y
print('Date difference:',diff)
```

The output from Listing A.9 is shown here:

```
Date difference: -210 days, 18:58:40.197130
```

EXCEPTION HANDLING IN PYTHON

Unlike `JavaScript` you cannot add a number and a string in `Python`. However, you can detect an illegal operation using the `try/except` construct in `Python`, which is similar to the `try/catch` construct in languages such as JavaScript and Java.

An example of a `try/except` block is here:

```
try:
   x = 4
   y = 'abc'
   z = x + y
except:
   print 'cannot add incompatible types:', x, y
```

When you run the preceding code in `Python`, the `print` statement in the `except` code block is executed because the variables x and y have incompatible types.

Earlier in the appendix you also saw that subtracting two strings throws an exception:

```
>>> 'a' - 'b'
Traceback (most recent call last):
  File "<stdin>", line 1, in <module>
TypeError: unsupported operand type(s) for -: 'str' and
'str'
```

A simple way to handle this situation is to use a try/except block:

```
>>> try:
...   print('a' - 'b')
... except TypeError:
...   print('TypeError exception while trying to
subtract two strings')
... except:
...   print('Exception while trying to subtract two
strings')
...
```

The output from the preceding code block is here:

```
TypeError exception while trying to subtract two
strings
```

As you can see, the preceding code block specifies the finer-grained exception called TypeError, followed by a "generic" except code block to handle all other exceptions that might occur during the execution of your Python code. This style is similar to the exception handling in Java code.

Listing A.10 displays the contents of Exception1.py that illustrates how to handle various types of exceptions.

Listing A.10: Exception1.py

```
import sys

try:
    f = open('myfile.txt')
    s = f.readline()
    i = int(s.strip())
```

```
except IOError as err:
    print("I/O error: {0}".format(err))
except ValueError:
    print("Could not convert data to an integer.")
except:
    print("Unexpected error:", sys.exc_info()[0])
    raise
```

Listing A.10 contains a `try` block followed by three `except` statements. If an error occurs in the `try` block, the first `except` statement is compared with the type of exception that occurred. If there is a match, then the subsequent `print()` statement is executed, and the program terminates. If not, a similar test is performed with the second `except` statement. If neither `except` statement matches the exception, the third `except` statement handles the exception, which involves printing a message and then "raising" an exception.

Note that you can also specify multiple exception types in a single statement, as shown here:

```
except (NameError, RuntimeError, TypeError):
    print('One of three error types occurred')
```

The preceding code block is more compact, but you do not know which of the three error types occurred. Python allows you to define custom exceptions, but this topic is beyond the scope of this book.

HANDLING USER INPUT

`Python` enables you to read user input from the command line via the `input()` function or the `raw_input()` function. Typically you assign user input to a variable, which will contain all characters that users enter from the keyboard. User input terminates when users press the <return> key (which is included with the input characters). Listing A.11 displays the contents of `UserInput1.py` that prompts users for their name and then uses interpolation to display a response.

Listing A.11: UserInput1.py

```
userInput = input("Enter your name: ")
print ("Hello %s, my name is Python" % userInput)
```

The output of Listing A.11 is here (assume that the user entered the word Dave):

```
Hello Dave, my name is Python
```

The `print()` statement in Listing A.11 uses string interpolation via `%s`, which substitutes the value of the variable after the `%` symbol. This functionality is obviously useful when you want to specify something that is determined at runtime.

User input can cause exceptions (depending on the operations that your code performs), so it's important to include exception-handling code.

Listing A.12 displays the contents of `UserInput2.py` that prompts users for a string and attempts to convert the string to a number in a `try/except` block.

Listing A.12: UserInput2.py

```
userInput = input("Enter something: ")


try:
  x = 0 + eval(userInput)
  print('you entered the number:',userInput)
except:
  print(userInput,'is a string')
```

Listing A.12 adds the number `0` to the result of converting a user's input to a number. If the conversion was successful, a message with the user's input is displayed. If the conversion failed, the `except` code block consists of a `print` statement that displays a message.

Note: this code sample uses the `eval()` function, which should be avoided so that your code does not evaluate arbitrary (and possibly destructive) commands.

Listing A.13 displays the contents of `UserInput3.py` that prompts users for two numbers and attempts to compute their sum in a pair of `try/except` blocks.

Listing A.13: UserInput3.py

```
sum = 0
```

```
msg = 'Enter a number:'
val1 = input(msg)


try:
  sum = sum + eval(val1)
except:
  print(val1,'is a string')

msg = 'Enter a number:'
val2 = input(msg)

try:
  sum = sum + eval(val2)
except:
  print(val2,'is a string')

print('The sum of',val1,'and',val2,'is',sum)
```

Listing A.13 contains two try blocks, each of which is followed by an except statement. The first try block attempts to add the first user-supplied number to the variable sum, and the second try block attempts to add the second user-supplied number to the previously entered number. An error message occurs if either input string is not a valid number; if both are valid numbers, a message is displayed containing the input numbers and their sum. Be sure to read the caveat regarding the eval() function that is mentioned earlier in this appendix.

PYTHON AND EMOJIS (OPTIONAL)

Listing A.14 displays the contents remove_emojis.py that illustrates how to remove emojis from a text string.

Listing A.14: remove_emojis.py

```
import re
import emoji
```

```
text = "I want a Chicago deep dish pizza tonight \
U0001f600"
print("text:")
print(text)
print()

emoji_pattern = re.compile("[" "\U0001F1E0-\U0001F6FF"
"]+", flags=re.UNICODE)
text = emoji_pattern.sub(r"", text)
text = "".join([x for x in text if x not in emoji.
UNICODE_EMOJI])
print("text:")
print(text)
print()
```

Listing A.14 starts with two `import` statements, followed by initializing the variable `text` with a text string, whose contents are displayed. The next portion of Listing A.14 defines the variable `emoji_pattern` as a regular expression that represents a range of Unicode values for emojis.

The next portion of Listing A.14 sets the variable `text` equal to the set of non emoji characters contained in the previously initialized value for `text` and then displays its contents. Launch the code in Listing A.14 and you will see the following output:

```
text:
I want a Chicago deep dish pizza tonight 😄

text:
I want a Chicago deep dish pizza tonight
```

COMMAND-LINE ARGUMENTS

`Python` provides a `getopt` module to parse command-line options and arguments, and the `Python sys` module provides access to any command-line arguments via the `sys.argv`. This serves two purposes:

* `sys.argv is the list of command-line arguments`
* `len(sys.argv) is the number of command-line arguments`

Here `sys.argv[0]` is the program name, so if the `Python` program is called `test.py`, it matches the value of `sys.argv[0]`.

Now you can provide input values for a `Python` program on the command line instead of providing input values by prompting users for their input.

As an example, consider the script `test.py` shown here:

```
#!/usr/bin/python
import sys
print('Number of arguments:',len(sys.argv),'arguments')
print('Argument List:', str(sys.argv))
```

Now run above script as follows:

```
python test.py arg1 arg2 arg3
```

This will produce following result:

```
Number of arguments: 4 arguments.
Argument List: ['test.py', 'arg1', 'arg2', 'arg3']
```

The ability to specify input values from the command line provides useful functionality. For example, suppose that you have a custom `Python` class that contains the methods `add` and `subtract` to add and subtract a pair of numbers.

You can use command-line arguments in order to specify which method to execute on a pair of numbers, as shown here:

```
python MyClass add 3 5
python MyClass subtract 3 5
```

This functionality is very useful because you can programmatically execute different methods in a `Python` class, which means that you can write unit tests for your code as well.

Listing A.15 displays the contents of `Hello.py` that shows you how to use `sys.argv` to check the number of command line parameters.

Listing A.15: Hello.py

```
import sys

def main():
  if len(sys.argv) >= 2:
    name = sys.argv[1]
```

```
else:
  name = 'World'
print('Hello', name)

# Standard boilerplate to invoke the main() function
if __name__ == '__main__':
  main()
```

Listing A.15 defines the main() function that checks the number of command-line parameters: if this value is at least 2, then the variable name is assigned the value of the second parameter (the first parameter is Hello.py), otherwise name is assigned the value Hello. The print statement then prints the value of the variable name.

The final portion of Listing A.15 uses conditional logic to determine whether or not to execute the main() function.

SUMMARY

This appendix showed you how to work with numbers and perform arithmetic operations on numbers, and then you learned how to work with strings and use string operations. Appendix B introduces you to data and how to perform various data-related operations.

INTRODUCTION TO PANDAS

This appendix introduces you to `Pandas` and provides code samples that illustrate some of its useful features. If you are familiar with these topics, skim through the material and peruse the code samples, just in case they contain information that is new to you.

The first part of this appendix contains a brief introduction to `Pandas`. This section contains code samples that illustrate some features of data frames and a brief discussion of series, which are two of the main features of `Pandas`.

The second part of this appendix discusses various types of data frames that you can create, such as numeric and `Boolean` data frames. In addition, we discuss examples of creating data frames with `NumPy` functions and random numbers.

Note: several code samples in this appendix reference the `NumPy` library for working with arrays and generating random numbers, which you can learn from online articles.

WHAT IS PANDAS?

`Pandas` is a `Python` package that is compatible with other `Python` packages, such as `NumPy` and `Matplotlib`. Install `Pandas` by opening a command shell and invoking this command for `Python` 3.x:

```
pip3 install pandas
```

In many ways, the semantics of the APIs in the `Pandas` library are similar to a spreadsheet, along with support for `xsl`, `xml`, `html`, and `csv` file types. `Pandas` provides a data type called a data frame (similar to a `Python` dictionary) with an extremely powerful functionality.

`Pandas` DataFrames support a variety of input types, such as `ndarray`, `list`, `dict`, or `series`.

The data type `series` is another mechanism for managing data. In addition to performing an online search for more details regarding `Series`, the following article contains a good introduction:

https://towardsdatascience.com/20-examples-to-master-pandas-series-bc4c68200324

Pandas Options and Settings

You can change the default values of environment variables, an example of which is shown below:

```
import pandas as pd


display_settings = {
    'max_columns': 8,
    'expand_frame_repr': True,  # Wrap to multiple
    pages
    'max_rows': 20,
    'precision': 3,
    'show_dimensions': True
}


for op, value in display_settings.items():
pd.set_option("display.{}".format(op), value)
```

Include the preceding code block in your own code if you want `Pandas` to display a maximum of twenty rows and eight columns, and floating point numbers displayed with three decimal places. Set `expand_frame_rep` to True if you want the output to "wrap around" to multiple pages. The preceding `for` loop iterates through `display_settings` and sets the options equal to their corresponding values.

In addition, the following code snippet displays all Pandas options and their current values in your code:

```
print(pd.describe_option())
```

There are various other operations that you can perform with options and their values (such as the `pd.reset()` method for resetting values), as described in the `Pandas` user guide:

https://pandas.pydata.org/pandas-docs/stable/user_guide/options.html

Pandas DataFrames

In simplified terms, a `Pandas` DataFrame is a two-dimensional data structure, and it's convenient to think of the data structure in terms of rows and columns. Data frames can be labeled (rows as well as columns), and the columns can contain different data types. The source of the dataset for a `Pandas` DataFrame can be a data file, a database table, and a Web service. The data frame features include

- data frame methods
- data frame statistics
- grouping, pivoting, and reshaping
- handle missing data
- join data frames

The code samples in this appendix show you almost all the features in the preceding list.

Data Frames and Data Cleaning Tasks

The specific tasks that you need to perform depend on the structure and contents of a dataset. In general, you will perform a workflow with the following steps, not necessarily always in this order (and some might be optional). All of the following steps can be performed with a `Pandas DataFrame`:

- read data into a data frame
- display top of data frame
- display column data types
- display missing values
- replace NA with a value
- iterate through the columns
- statistics for each column
- find missing values
- total missing values
- percentage of missing values
- sort table values
- print summary information
- columns with > 50% missing
- rename columns

This appendix contains sections that illustrate how to perform many of the steps in the preceding list.

Alternatives to Pandas

Before delving into the code samples, there are alternatives to Pandas that offer very useful features, some of which are shown here:

- PySpark (for large datasets)
- Dask (for distributed processing)
- Modin (faster performance)
- Datatable (R data.table for Python)

The inclusion of these alternatives is not intended to diminish Pandas. Indeed, you might not need any of the functionality in the preceding list. However, you might need such functionality in the future, so it's worthwhile for you to know about these alternatives now (and there may be even more powerful alternatives at some point in the future).

A PANDAS DATAFRAME WITH A NUMPY EXAMPLE

Listing B.1 shows the content of pandas_df.py that illustrates how to define several data frames and display their contents.

Listing B.1: pandas_df.py

```
import pandas as pd
import numpy as np

myvector1 = np.array([1,2,3,4,5])
print("myvector1:")
print(myvector1)
print()

mydf1 = pd.Data frame(myvector1)
print("mydf1:")
print(mydf1)
print()

myvector2 = np.array([i for i in range(1,6)])
print("myvector2:")
```

```
print(myvector2)
print()


mydf2 = pd.Data frame(myvector2)
print("mydf2:")
print(mydf2)
print()


myarray = np.array([[10,30,20],
[50,40,60],[1000,2000,3000]])
print("myarray:")
print(myarray)
print()


mydf3 = pd.Data frame(myarray)
print("mydf3:")
print(mydf3)
print()
```

Listing B.1 starts with standard `import` statements for `Pandas` and `NumPy`, followed by the definition of two one-dimensional `NumPy` arrays and a two-dimensional `NumPy` array. Each `NumPy` variable is followed by a corresponding `Pandas DataFrame` (`mydf1`, `mydf2`, and `mydf3`). Launch the code in Listing B.1 to see the following output, and you can compare the `NumPy` arrays with the `Pandas DataFrames`:

```
myvector1:
[1 2 3 4 5]


mydf1:
   0
0  1
1  2
2  3
3  4
4  5
```

```
myvector2:
[1 2 3 4 5]

mydf2:
   0
0  1
1  2
2  3
3  4
4  5

myarray:
[[   10    30    20]
 [   50    40    60]
 [1000 2000 3000]]

mydf3:
      0     1     2
0    10    30    20
1    50    40    60
2  1000  2000  3000
```

By contrast, the following code block illustrates how to define two Pandas Series that are part of the definition of a Pandas DataFrame:

```
names = pd.Series(['SF', 'San Jose', 'Sacramento'])
sizes = pd.Series([852469, 1015785, 485199])
df = pd.Data frame({ 'Cities': names, 'Size': sizes })
print(df)
```

Create a Python file with the preceding code (along with the required import statement), and when you launch that code, you will see the following output:

```
     City name      sizes
0           SF     852469
1     San Jose    1015785
2   Sacramento     485199
```

DESCRIBING A PANDAS DATAFRAME

Listing B.2 shows the content of `pandas_df_describe.py`, which illustrates how to define a `Pandas` DataFrame that contains a 3x3 `NumPy` array of integer values, where the rows and columns of the data frame are labeled. Other aspects of the data frame are also displayed.

Listing B.2: pandas_df_describe.py

```
import numpy as np
import pandas as pd

myarray = np.array([[10,30,20],
[50,40,60],[1000,2000,3000]])

rownames = ['apples', 'oranges', 'beer']
colnames = ['January', 'February', 'March']

mydf = pd.Data frame(myarray, index=rownames,
columns=colnames)
print("contents of df:")
print(mydf)
print()

print("contents of January:")
print(mydf['January'])
print()

print("Number of Rows:")
print(mydf.shape[0])
print()

print("Number of Columns:")
print(mydf.shape[1])
print()
```

```
print("Number of Rows and Columns:")
print(mydf.shape)
print()

print("Column Names:")
print(mydf.columns)
print()

print("Column types:")
print(mydf.dtypes)
print()

print("Description:")
print(mydf.describe())
print()
```

Listing B.2 starts with two standard `import` statements followed by the variable `myarray`, which is a 3x3 `NumPy` array of numbers. The variables `rownames` and `colnames` provide names for the rows and columns, respectively, of the `Pandas DataFrame mydf`, which is initialized as a `Pandas` Data-Frame with the specified data source (i.e., `myarray`).

The first portion of the following output requires a single `print()` statement (which simply displays the contents of `mydf`). The second portion of the output is generated by invoking the `describe()` method that is available for any `Pandas` DataFrame. The `describe()` method is useful: you will see various statistical quantities, such as the mean, standard deviation minimum, and maximum performed by *columns* (not rows), along with values for the 25th, 50th, and 75th percentiles. The output of Listing B.2 is here:

```
contents of df:
         January  February  March
apples        10        30     20
oranges       50        40     60
beer        1000      2000   3000

contents of January:
apples        10
```

```
oranges       50
beer        1000
Name: January, dtype: int64
```

```
Number of Rows:
3
```

```
Number of Columns:
3
```

```
Number of Rows and Columns:
(3, 3)
```

```
Column Names:
Index(['January', 'February', 'March'], dtype='object')
```

```
Column types:
January      int64
February     int64
March        int64
dtype: object
```

```
Description:
            January     February        March
count      3.000000     3.000000     3.000000
mean     353.333333   690.000000  1026.666667
std      560.386771  1134.504297  1709.073823
min       10.000000    30.000000    20.000000
25%       30.000000    35.000000    40.000000
50%       50.000000    40.000000    60.000000
75%      525.000000  1020.000000  1530.000000
max     1000.000000  2000.000000  3000.000000
```

PANDAS BOOLEAN DATAFRAMES

`Pandas` supports Boolean operations on data frames, such as the logical `OR`, the logical `AND`, and the logical negation of a pair of `Data frames`. Listing B.3 shows the content of `pandas_boolean_df.py` that illustrates how to define a `Pandas` DataFrame whose rows and columns are `Boolean` values.

Listing B.3: pandas_boolean_df.py

```
import pandas as pd

df1 = pd.Data frame({'a': [1, 0, 1], 'b': [0, 1, 1] },
dtype=bool)
df2 = pd.Data frame({'a': [0, 1, 1], 'b': [1, 1, 0] },
dtype=bool)

print("df1 & df2:")
print(df1 & df2)

print("df1 | df2:")
print(df1 | df2)

print("df1 ^ df2:")
print(df1 ^ df2)
```

Listing B.3 initializes the `data frames df1` and `df2`, and then computes `df1 & df2`, `df1 | df2`, and `df1 ^ df2`, which represent the logical `AND`, the logical `OR`, and the logical negation, respectively, of `df1` and `df2`. The output from launching the code in Listing B.3 is as follows:

```
df1 & df2:
        a       b
0   False   False
1   False    True
2    True   False
df1 | df2:
        a       b
0    True    True
1    True    True
```

```
2   True   True
df1 ^ df2:
        a       b
0    True    True
1    True    False
2    False    True
```

Transposing a Pandas DataFrame

The T attribute (as well as the transpose function) enables you to generate the transpose of a Pandas DataFrame, similar to the NumPy ndarray. The transpose operation switches rows to columns and columns to rows. For example, the following code snippet defines a Pandas DataFrame df1 and then displays the transpose of df1:

```
df1 = pd.Data frame({'a': [1, 0, 1], 'b': [0, 1, 1] },
dtype=int)

print("df1.T:")
print(df1.T)
```

The output of the preceding code snippet is here:

```
df1.T:
    0   1   2
a   1   0   1
b   0   1   1
```

The following code snippet defines Pandas DataFrames df1 and df2 and then displays their sum:

```
df1 = pd.Data frame({'a' : [1, 0, 1], 'b' : [0, 1, 1]
}, dtype=int)
df2 = pd.Data frame({'a' : [3, 3, 3], 'b' : [5, 5, 5]
}, dtype=int)

print("df1 + df2:")
print(df1 + df2)
```

```
The output is here:
df1 + df2:
   a  b
0  4  5
1  3  6
2  4  6
```

PANDAS DATAFRAMES AND RANDOM NUMBERS

Listing B.4 shows the content of pandas_random_df.py that illustrates how to create a Pandas DataFrame with random integers.

Listing B.4: pandas_random_df.py

```
import pandas as pd
import numpy as np

df = pd.Data frame(np.random.randint(1, 5, size=(5,
2)), columns=['a','b'])
df = df.append(df.agg(['sum', 'mean']))

print("Contents of data frame:")
print(df)
```

Listing B.4 defines the Pandas DataFrame df that consists of 5 rows and 2 columns of random integers between 1 and 5. Notice that the columns of df are labeled "a" and "b." In addition, the next code snippet appends two rows consisting of the sum and the mean of the numbers in both columns. The output of Listing B.4 is here:

```
      a     b
0     1.0   2.0
1     1.0   1.0
2     4.0   3.0
3     3.0   1.0
4     1.0   2.0
sum   10.0  9.0
mean  2.0   1.8
```

Listing B.5 shows the content of `pandas_combine_df.py` that illustrates how to combine Pandas `DataFrames`.

Listing B.5: pandas_combine_df.py

```
import pandas as pd
import numpy as np

df = pd.Data frame({'foo1' : np.random.randn(5),
                    'foo2' : np.random.randn(5)})

print("contents of df:")
print(df)

print("contents of foo1:")
print(df.foo1)

print("contents of foo2:")
print(df.foo2)
```

Listing B.3 initializes the `data frames` df1 and df2, and then computes df1 & df2, df1 | df2, and df1 ^ df2, which represent the logical AND, the logical OR, and the logical negation, respectively, of df1 and df2. The output from launching the code in Listing B.3 is as follows:

```
contents of df:
        foo1       foo2
0   0.274680 -0.848669
1  -0.399771 -0.814679
2   0.454443 -0.363392
3   0.473753  0.550849
4  -0.211783 -0.015014
contents of foo1:
0      0.256773
1      1.204322
2      1.040515
3     -0.518414
4      0.634141
```

```
Name: foo1, dtype: float64
contents of foo2:
0    -2.506550
1    -0.896516
2    -0.222923
3     0.934574
4     0.527033
Name: foo2, dtype: float64
```

READING CSV FILES IN PANDAS

Pandas provides the `read_csv()` method for reading the contents of CSV files. For example, Listing B.6 shows the contents of `sometext.csv` that contain labeled data (`spam` or `ham`), and Listing B.7 shows the contents of `read_csv_file.py` that illustrates how to read the contents of a CSV file.

Listing B.6: sometext.csv

```
type      text
ham       Available only for today
ham       I'm joking with you
spam      Free entry in 2 a wkly comp
ham       U dun say so early hor
ham       I don't think he goes to usf
spam      FreeMsg Hey there
ham       my brother is not sick
ham       As per your request Melle
spam      WINNER!! As a valued customer
```

Listing B.7: read_csv_file.py

```python
import pandas as pd
import numpy as np

df = pd.read_csv('sometext.csv', delimiter='\t')
```

```
print("=> First five rows:")
print(df.head(5))
```

Listing B.7 reads the contents of `sometext.csv`, and the columns are separated by a tab ("\t") delimiter. Launch the code in Listing B.7 to see the following output:

```
=> First five rows:
    type                          text
0   ham       Available only for today
1   ham                I'm joking with you
2   spam   Free entry in 2 a wkly comp
3   ham           U dun say so early hor
4   ham   I don't think he goes to usf
```

The default value for the `head()` method is 5, but you can display the first n rows of a data frame `df` with the code snippet `df.head(n)`.

Specifying a Separator and Column Sets in Text Files

The previous section showed you how to use the `delimiter` attribute to specify the delimiter in a text file. You can also use the `sep` parameter specifies a different separator. In addition, you can assign the `names` parameter the column names in the data that you want to read. An example of using `delimiter` and `sep` is here:

```
df2 = pd.read_csv("data.csv",sep="|",
                  names=["Name","Surname","Height","We
                  ight"])
```

`Pandas` also provides the `read_table()` method for reading the contents of CSV files, which uses the same syntax as the `read_csv()` method.

Specifying an Index in Text Files

Suppose that you know that a particular column in a text file contains the index value for the rows in the text file. For example, a text file that contains the data in a relational table would typically contain an index column.

Fortunately, `Pandas` allows you to specify the kth column as the index in a text file, as shown here:

```
df = pd.read_csv('myfile.csv', index_col=k)
```

THE LOC() AND ILOC() METHODS IN PANDAS

If you want to display the contents of a record in a `Pandas` DataFrame, specify the index of the row in the `loc()` method. For example, the following code snippet displays the data by feature name in a data frame `df`:

```
df.loc[feature_name]
```

Select the first row of the "height" column in the data frame:

```
df.loc([0], ['height'])
```

The following code snippet uses the `iloc()` function to display the first 8 records of the name column with this code snippet:

```
df.iloc[0:8]['name']
```

CONVERTING CATEGORICAL DATA TO NUMERIC DATA

One common task (especially in machine learning) involves converting a feature containing character data into a feature that contains numeric data. Listing B.8 shows the contents of `cat2numeric.py` that illustrate how to replace a text field with a corresponding numeric field.

Listing B.8: cat2numeric.py

```
import pandas as pd
import numpy as np

df = pd.read_csv('sometext.csv', delimiter='\t')

print("=> First five rows (before):")
print(df.head(5))
print("------------------------")
print()

# map ham/spam to 0/1 values:
df['type'] = df['type'].map( {'ham':0 , 'spam':1} )
```

```
print("=> First five rows (after):")
print(df.head(5))
print("-------------------------")
```

Listing B.8 initializes the data frame `df` with the contents of the `csv` file `sometext.csv`, and then displays the contents of the first five rows by invoking `df.head(5)`, which is also the default number of rows to display.

The next code snippet in Listing B.8 invokes the `map()` method to replace occurrences of `ham` with 0 and replace occurrences of `spam` with 1 in the column labeled `type`, as shown here:

```
df['type'] = df['type'].map( {'ham':0 , 'spam':1} )
```

The last portion of Listing B.8 invokes the `head()` method again to display the first five rows of the dataset after having renamed the contents of the column type. Launch the code in Listing B.8 to see the following output:

```
=> First five rows (before):
    type                       text
0   ham      Available only for today
1   ham             I'm joking with you
2   spam  Free entry in 2 a wkly comp
3   ham           U dun say so early hor
4   ham   I don't think he goes to usf
-------------------------


=> First five rows (after):
    type                       text
0    0       Available only for today
1    0              I'm joking with you
2    1   Free entry in 2 a wkly comp
3    0            U dun say so early hor
4    0   I don't think he goes to usf


-------------------------
```

As another example, Listing B.9 shows the contents of `shirts.csv` and Listing B.10 shows the contents of `shirts.py`; these examples illustrate four techniques for converting categorical data into numeric data.

Listing B.9: shirts.csv

```
type,ssize
shirt,xxlarge
shirt,xxlarge
shirt,xlarge
shirt,xlarge
shirt,xlarge
shirt,large
shirt,medium
shirt,small
shirt,small
shirt,xsmall
shirt,xsmall
shirt,xsmall
```

Listing B.10: shirts.py

```python
import pandas as pd

shirts = pd.read_csv("shirts.csv")
print("shirts before:")
print(shirts)
print()

# TECHNIQUE #1:
#shirts.loc[shirts['ssize']=='xxlarge','size'] = 4
#shirts.loc[shirts['ssize']=='xlarge', 'size'] = 4
#shirts.loc[shirts['ssize']=='large',  'size'] = 3
#shirts.loc[shirts['ssize']=='medium', 'size'] = 2
#shirts.loc[shirts['ssize']=='small',  'size'] = 1
#shirts.loc[shirts['ssize']=='xsmall', 'size'] = 1

# TECHNIQUE #2:
#shirts['ssize'].replace('xxlarge', 4, inplace=True)
#shirts['ssize'].replace('xlarge',  4, inplace=True)
```

```
#shirts['ssize'].replace('large',   3, inplace=True)
#shirts['ssize'].replace('medium',  2, inplace=True)
#shirts['ssize'].replace('small',   1, inplace=True)
#shirts['ssize'].replace('xsmall',  1, inplace=True)

# TECHNIQUE #3:
#shirts['ssize'] = shirts['ssize'].apply({'xxlarge':4,
'xlarge':4, 'large':3, 'medium':2, 'small':1,
'xsmall':1}.get)

# TECHNIQUE #4:
shirts['ssize'] = shirts['ssize'].
replace(regex='xlarge', value=4)
shirts['ssize'] = shirts['ssize'].
replace(regex='large',  value=3)
shirts['ssize'] = shirts['ssize'].
replace(regex='medium', value=2)
shirts['ssize'] = shirts['ssize'].
replace(regex='small',  value=1)

print("shirts after:")
print(shirts)
```

Listing B.10 starts with a code block of six statements that uses direct comparison with strings to make numeric replacements. For example, the following code snippet replaces all occurrences of the string xxlarge with the value 4:

```
shirts.loc[shirts['ssize']=='xxlarge','size'] = 4
```

The second code block consists of six statements that use the replace() method to perform the same updates, an example of which is shown here:

```
shirts['ssize'].replace('xxlarge', 4, inplace=True)
```

The third code block consists of a single statement that uses the apply() method to perform the same updates, as shown here:

```
shirts['ssize'] = shirts['ssize'].apply({'xxlarge':4,
'xlarge':4, 'large':3, 'medium':2, 'small':1,
'xsmall':1}.get)
```

The fourth code block consists of four statements that use regular expressions to perform the same updates, an example of which is shown here:

```
shirts['ssize'] = shirts['ssize'].
replace(regex='xlarge', value=4)
```

Since the preceding code snippet matches xxlarge as well as xlarge, we only need *four* statements instead of six statements. (If you are unfamiliar with regular expressions, you can read the relevant appendix.) Now launch the code in Listing B.10 to see the following output:

```
shirts before
        type      size
0      shirt    xxlarge
1      shirt    xxlarge
2      shirt     xlarge
3      shirt     xlarge
4      shirt     xlarge
5      shirt      large
6      shirt     medium
7      shirt      small
8      shirt      small
9      shirt     xsmall
10     shirt     xsmall
11     shirt     xsmall

shirts after:
        type    size
0      shirt     4
1      shirt     4
2      shirt     4
3      shirt     4
4      shirt     4
5      shirt     3
6      shirt     2
7      shirt     1
8      shirt     1
9      shirt     1
```

```
10   shirt       1
11   shirt       1
```

MATCHING AND SPLITTING STRINGS IN PANDAS

Listing B.11 shows the content of shirts_str.py, which illustrates how to match a column value with an initial string and how to split a column value based on a letter.

Listing B.11: shirts_str.py

```
import pandas as pd

shirts = pd.read_csv("shirts2.csv")
print("shirts:")
print(shirts)
print()

print("shirts starting with xl:")
print(shirts[shirts.ssize.str.startswith('xl')])
print()

print("Exclude 'xlarge' shirts:")
print(shirts[shirts['ssize'] != 'xlarge'])
print()

print("first three letters:")
shirts['sub1'] = shirts['ssize'].str[:3]
print(shirts)
print()

print("split ssize on letter 'a':")
shirts['sub2'] = shirts['ssize'].str.split('a')
print(shirts)
print()
```

```
print("Rows 3 through 5 and column 2:")
print(shirts.iloc[2:5, 2])
print()
```

Listing B.11 initializes the data frame df with the contents of the csv file shirts.csv, and then displays the contents of df. The next code snippet in Listing B.11 uses the startswith() method to match the shirt types that start with the letters xl, followed by a code snippet that displays the shorts whose size does not equal the string xlarge.

The next code snippet uses the construct str[:3] to display the first three letters of the shirt types, followed by a code snippet that uses the split() method to split the shirt types based on the letter "a."

The final code snippet invokes iloc[2:5,2] to display the contents of rows 3 through 5 inclusive, and only the second column. The output of Listing B.11 is as follows:

```
shirts:
        type     ssize
0      shirt   xxlarge
1      shirt   xxlarge
2      shirt    xlarge
3      shirt    xlarge
4      shirt    xlarge
5      shirt     large
6      shirt    medium
7      shirt     small
8      shirt     small
9      shirt    xsmall
10     shirt    xsmall
11     shirt    xsmall

shirts starting with xl:
      type     ssize
2    shirt   xlarge
3    shirt   xlarge
4    shirt   xlarge
```

Exclude 'xlarge' shirts:

	type	ssize
0	shirt	xxlarge
1	shirt	xxlarge
5	shirt	large
6	shirt	medium
7	shirt	small
8	shirt	small
9	shirt	xsmall
10	shirt	xsmall
11	shirt	xsmall

first three letters:

	type	ssize	sub1
0	shirt	xxlarge	xxl
1	shirt	xxlarge	xxl
2	shirt	xlarge	xla
3	shirt	xlarge	xla
4	shirt	xlarge	xla
5	shirt	large	lar
6	shirt	medium	med
7	shirt	small	sma
8	shirt	small	sma
9	shirt	xsmall	xsm
10	shirt	xsmall	xsm
11	shirt	xsmall	xsm

split ssize on letter 'a':

	type	ssize	sub1	sub2
0	shirt	xxlarge	xxl	[xxl, rge]
1	shirt	xxlarge	xxl	[xxl, rge]
2	shirt	xlarge	xla	[xl, rge]
3	shirt	xlarge	xla	[xl, rge]
4	shirt	xlarge	xla	[xl, rge]

```
5      shirt      large   lar    [l, rge]
6      shirt      medium  med    [medium]
7      shirt      small   sma    [sm, ll]
8      shirt      small   sma    [sm, ll]
9      shirt      xsmall  xsm    [xsm, ll]
10     shirt      xsmall  xsm    [xsm, ll]
11     shirt      xsmall  xsm    [xsm, ll]


Rows 3 through 5 and column 2:
2      xlarge
3      xlarge
4      xlarge
Name: ssize, dtype: object
```

CONVERTING STRINGS TO DATES IN PANDAS

Listing B.12 shows the content of string2date.py, which illustrates how to convert strings to date formats.

Listing B.12: string2date.py

```
import pandas as pd

bdates1 = {'strdates':  ['20210413','20210813','202112
25'],
          'people': ['Sally','Steve','Sarah']
          }

df1 = pd.Data frame(bdates1, columns =
['strdates','people'])
df1['dates'] = pd.to_datetime(df1['strdates'],
format='%Y%m%d')
print("=> Contents of data frame df1:")
print(df1)
print()
print(df1.dtypes)
print()
```

```
bdates2 = {'strdates':  ['13Apr2021','08Aug2021','25D
ec2021'],
          'people': ['Sally','Steve','Sarah']
          }

df2 = pd.Data frame(bdates2, columns =
['strdates','people'])
df2['dates'] = pd.to_datetime(df2['strdates'],
format='%d%b%Y')
print("=> Contents of data frame df2:")
print(df2)
print()


print(df2.dtypes)
print()
```

Listing B.12 initializes the data frame df1 with the contents of bdates1, and then converts the strdates column to dates using the %Y%m%d format. The next portion of Listing B.12 initializes the data frame df2 with the contents of bdates2, and then converts the strdates column to dates using the %d%b%Y format. Launch the code in Listing B.12 to see the following output:

```
=> Contents of data frame df1:
   strdates people       dates
0  20210413  Sally 2021-04-13
1  20210813  Steve 2021-08-13
2  20211225  Sarah 2021-12-25

strdates               object
people                 object
dates          datetime64[ns]
dtype: object

=> Contents of data frame df2:
    strdates people       dates
0  13Apr2021  Sally 2021-04-13
1  08Aug2021  Steve 2021-08-08
2  25Dec2021  Sarah 2021-12-25
```

```
strdates            object
people              object
dates        datetime64[ns]
dtype: object
```

WORKING WITH DATE RANGES IN PANDAS

Listing B.13 shows the content of pand_parse_dates.py that shows how to work with date ranges in a CSV file.

Listing B.13: pand_parse_dates.py

```python
import pandas as pd

df = pd.read_csv('multiple_dates.csv', parse_
dates=['dates'])

print("df:")
print(df)
print()

df = df.set_index(['dates'])
start_d = "2021-04-30"
end_d   = "2021-08-31"

print("DATES BETWEEN",start_d,"AND",end_d,":")
print(df.loc[start_d:end_d])
print()

print("DATES BEFORE",start_d,":")
print(df.loc[df.index < start_d])

years = ['2020','2021','2022']
for year in years:
  year_sum = df.loc[year].sum()[0]
  print("SUM OF VALUES FOR YEAR",year,":",year_sum)
```

Listing B.13 starts by initializing the variable df with the contents of the CSV file `multiple_dates.csv` and then displaying its contents. The next code snippet sets the dates column as the index column and then initializes the variable `start_d` and `end_d` that contain a start date and an end date, respectively.

The next portion of Listing B.13 displays the dates between `start_d` and `end_d`, and then the list of dates that precede `start_d`. The final code block iterates through a list of years and then calculates the sum of the numbers in the values field for each year in the list. Launch the code in Listing B.13 to see the following output:

```
df:
         dates   values
0   2020-01-31    40.0
1   2020-02-28    45.0
2   2020-03-31    56.0
3   2021-04-30     NaN
4   2021-05-31     NaN
5   2021-06-30   140.0
6   2021-07-31    95.0
7   2022-08-31    40.0
8   2022-09-30    55.0
9   2022-10-31     NaN
10  2022-11-15    65.0


DATES BETWEEN 2021-04-30 AND 2021-08-31 :
              values
dates
2021-04-30      NaN
2021-05-31      NaN
2021-06-30    140.0
2021-07-31     95.0


DATES BEFORE 2021-04-30 :
              values
dates
2020-01-31     40.0
```

```
2020-02-28      45.0
2020-03-31      56.0

SUM OF VALUES FOR YEAR 2020 : 141.0
SUM OF VALUES FOR YEAR 2021 : 235.0
SUM OF VALUES FOR YEAR 2022 : 160.0
```

DETECTING MISSING DATES IN PANDAS

Listing B.14 shows the contents of pandas_missing_dates.py that shows how to detect missing date values in a CSV file.

Listing B.14: pandas_missing_dates.py

```
import pandas as pd

# A data frame from a dictionary of lists
data = {'Date': ['2021-01-18', '2021-01-20', '2021-01-
21', '2021-01-24'],
        'Name': ['Joe', 'John', 'Jane', 'Jim']}
df = pd.Data frame(data)

# Setting the Date values as index:
df = df.set_index('Date')

# to_datetime() converts string format to a DateTime
object:
df.index = pd.to_datetime(df.index)

start_d="2021-01-18"
end_d="2021-01-25"

# display dates that are not in the sequence:
print("MISSING DATES BETWEEN",start_d,"and",end_d,":")
dates = pd.date_range(start=start_d, end=end_d).
difference(df.index)
```

```
for date in dates:
  print("date:",date)
print()
```

Listing B.14 initializes the dictionary `data` with a list of values for the `Date` field and the `Name` field, after which the variable `df` is initialized as a data frame whose contents are from the `data` variable.

The next code snippet sets the `Date` field as the index of the data frame `df`, after which the string-based dates are converted to `DateTime` objects. Another pair of code snippets initialize the variable `start_d` and `end_d` with a start date and an end date, respectively.

The final portion of Listing B.14 initializes the variable `dates` with the list of missing dates between `start_d` and `end_d`, after which the contents of `dates` are displayed. Launch the code in Listing B.14 to see the following output:

```
MISSING DATES BETWEEN 2021-01-18 and 2021-01-25 :
date: 2022-01-19 00:00:00
date: 2022-01-22 00:00:00
date: 2022-01-23 00:00:00
date: 2022-01-25 00:00:00
```

INTERPOLATING MISSING DATES IN PANDAS

Listing B.15 shows the contents of `missing_dates.csv` and Listing B.16 shows the contents of `pandas_interpolate.py` that shows how to replace `NaN` values with interpolated values that are calculated in several ways.

Listing B.15: missing_dates.csv

```
"dates","values"
2021-01-31,40
2021-02-28,45
2021-03-31,56
2021-04-30,NaN
2021-05-31,NaN
2021-06-30,140
2021-07-31,95
2021-08-31,40
```

```
2021-09-30,55
2021-10-31,NaN
2021-11-15,65
```

Notice the value 140 (shown in bold) in Listing B.15: this value is an outlier, which will affect the calculation of the interpolated values, and potentially generate additional outliers.

Listing B.16: pandas_interpolate.py

```
import pandas as pd
df = pd.read_csv("missing_dates.csv")

# fill NaN values with linear interpolation:
df1 = df.interpolate()

# fill NaN values with quadratic polynomial
interpolation:
df2 = df.interpolate(method='polynomial', order=2)

# fill NaN values with cubic polynomial interpolation:
df3 = df.interpolate(method='polynomial', order=3)

print("original data frame:")
print(df)
print()
print("linear interpolation:")
print(df1)
print()
print("quadratic interpolation:")
print(df2)
print()
print("cubic interpolation:")
print(df3)
print()
```

Listing B.16 initializes `df` with the contents of the CSV file `missing_dates.csv` and then initializes the three data frames `df1`, `df2`, and `df3` that are based on linear, quadratic, and cubic interpolation, respectively, via the `interpolate()` method. Now launch the code in Listing B.16 to see the following output:

```
original data frame:
        dates   values
0   2021-01-31    40.0
1   2021-02-28    45.0
2   2021-03-31    56.0
3   2021-04-30     NaN
4   2021-05-31     NaN
5   2021-06-30   140.0
6   2021-07-31    95.0
7   2021-08-31    40.0
8   2021-09-30    55.0
9   2021-10-31     NaN
10  2021-11-15    65.0

linear interpolation:
        dates   values
0   2021-01-31    40.0
1   2021-02-28    45.0
2   2021-03-31    56.0
3   2021-04-30    84.0
4   2021-05-31   112.0
5   2021-06-30   140.0
6   2021-07-31    95.0
7   2021-08-31    40.0
8   2021-09-30    55.0
9   2021-10-31    60.0
10  2021-11-15    65.0
```

```
quadratic interpolation:
          dates       values
0    2021-01-31    40.000000
1    2021-02-28    45.000000
2    2021-03-31    56.000000
3    2021-04-30    88.682998
4    2021-05-31   136.002883
5    2021-06-30   140.000000
6    2021-07-31    95.000000
7    2021-08-31    40.000000
8    2021-09-30    55.000000
9    2021-10-31    68.162292
10   2021-11-15    65.000000

cubic interpolation:
          dates       values
0    2021-01-31    40.000000
1    2021-02-28    45.000000
2    2021-03-31    56.000000
3    2021-04-30    92.748096
4    2021-05-31   132.055687
5    2021-06-30   140.000000
6    2021-07-31    95.000000
7    2021-08-31    40.000000
8    2021-09-30    55.000000
9    2021-10-31    91.479905
10   2021-11-15    65.000000
```

OTHER OPERATIONS WITH DATES IN PANDAS

Listing B.17 shows the contents of `pandas_misc1.py` that shows how to extract a list of years from a column in a data frame.

Listing B.17: pandas_misc1.py

```
import pandas as pd
import numpy as np

df = pd.read_csv('multiple_dates.csv', parse_
dates=['dates'])
print("df:")
print(df)
print()

year_list = df['dates']

arr1 = np.array([])
for long_year in year_list:
  year = str(long_year)
  short_year = year[0:4]
  arr1 = np.append(arr1,short_year)

unique_years = set(arr1)
print("unique_years:")
print(unique_years)
print()

unique_arr = np.array(pd.Data frame.from_dict(unique_
years))
print("unique_arr:")
print(unique_arr)
print()
```

Listing B.17 initializes df with the contents of the CSV file multiple_
dates.csv and then displays its contents. The next portion of Listing B.17
initializes year_list with the dates column of df.

The next code block contains a loop that iterates through the elements in
year_list, extracts the first four characters (i.e., the year value) and appends
that substring to the NumPy array arr1. The final code block initializes the

variable `unique_arr` as a `Numpy` array consisting of the unique years in the dictionary `unique_years`. Launch the code in Listing B.17 to see the following output:

```
df:
         dates   values
0   2020-01-31    40.0
1   2020-02-28    45.0
2   2020-03-31    56.0
3   2021-04-30     NaN
4   2021-05-31     NaN
5   2021-06-30   140.0
6   2021-07-31    95.0
7   2022-08-31    40.0
8   2022-09-30    55.0
9   2022-10-31     NaN
10  2022-11-15    65.0

unique_years:
{'2022', '2020', '2021'}

unique_arr:
[['2022']
 ['2020']
 ['2021']]
```

Listing B.18 shows the contents of `pandas_misc2.py` that shows how to iterate through the rows of a data frame. Keep in mind that row-wise iteration is not recommended because it can result in performance issues in larger datasets.

Listing B.18: pandas_misc2.py

```
import pandas as pd

df = pd.read_csv('multiple_dates.csv', parse_
dates=['dates'])
```

```
print("df:")
print(df)
print()

print("=> ITERATE THROUGH THE ROWS:")
for idx,row in df.iterrows():
  print("idx:",idx," year:",row['dates'])
print()
```

Listing B.18 initializes the `Pandas DataFrame df`, prints its contents, and then processes the rows of `df` in a loop. During each iteration, the current index and row contents are displayed. Now launch the code in Listing B.18 to see the following output:

```
df:
       dates   values
0   2020-01-31    40.0
1   2020-02-28    45.0
2   2020-03-31    56.0
3   2021-04-30     NaN
4   2021-05-31     NaN
5   2021-06-30   140.0
6   2021-07-31    95.0
7   2022-08-31    40.0
8   2022-09-30    55.0
9   2022-10-31     NaN
10  2022-11-15    65.0

=> ITERATE THROUGH THE ROWS:
idx:  0   year:  2020-01-31 00:00:00
idx:  1   year:  2020-02-28 00:00:00
idx:  2   year:  2020-03-31 00:00:00
idx:  3   year:  2021-04-30 00:00:00
idx:  4   year:  2021-05-31 00:00:00
idx:  5   year:  2021-06-30 00:00:00
idx:  6   year:  2021-07-31 00:00:00
```

```
idx: 7   year: 2022-08-31 00:00:00
idx: 8   year: 2022-09-30 00:00:00
idx: 9   year: 2022-10-31 00:00:00
idx: 10  year: 2022-11-15 00:00:00
```

Listing B.19 shows the contents of `pandas_misc3.py` that shows how to display a weekly set of dates that are between a start date and an end date.

Listing B.19: pandas_misc3.py

```
import pandas as pd

start_d="01/02/2022"
end_d="12/02/2022"
weekly_dates=pd.date_range(start=start_d, end=end_d,
freq='W')

print("Weekly dates from",start_d,"to",end_d,":")
print(weekly_dates)
```

Listing B.19 starts with initializing the variable `start_d` and `end_d` that contain a start date and an end date, respectively, and then initializes the variable `weekly_dates` with a list of weekly dates between the start date and the end date. Now launch the code in Listing B.19 to see the following output:

```
Weekly dates from 01/02/2022 to 12/02/2022 :
DatetimeIndex(['2022-01-02', '2022-01-09',
'2022-01-16', '2022-01-23',
               '2022-01-30', '2022-02-06',
               '2022-02-13', '2022-02-20',
               '2022-02-27', '2022-03-06',
               '2022-03-13', '2022-03-20',
               '2022-03-27', '2022-04-03',
               '2022-04-10', '2022-04-17',
               '2022-04-24', '2022-05-01',
               '2022-05-08', '2022-05-15',
               '2022-05-22', '2022-05-29',
               '2022-06-05', '2022-06-12',
               '2022-06-19', '2022-06-26',
               '2022-07-03', '2022-07-10',
               '2022-07-17', '2022-07-24',
               '2022-07-31', '2022-08-07',
```

```
'2022-08-14', '2022-08-21', '2022-08-
28', '2022-09-04',
'2022-09-11', '2022-09-18', '2022-09-
25', '2022-10-02',
'2022-10-09', '2022-10-16', '2022-10-
23', '2022-10-30',
'2022-11-06', '2022-11-13', '2022-11-
20', '2022-11-27'],
dtype='datetime64[ns]', freq='W-SUN')
```

MERGING AND SPLITTING COLUMNS IN PANDAS

Listing B.20 shows the contents of employees.csv and Listing B.21 shows the contents of emp_merge_split.py; these examples illustrate how to merge columns and split columns of a CSV file.

Listing B.20: employees.csv

```
name,year,month
Jane-Smith,2015,Aug
Dave-Smith,2020,Jan
Jane-Jones,2018,Dec
Jane-Stone,2017,Feb
Dave-Stone,2014,Apr
Mark-Aster,,Oct
Jane-Jones,NaN,Jun
```

Listing B.21: emp_merge_split.py

```
import pandas as pd

emps = pd.read_csv("employees.csv")
print("emps:")
print(emps)
print()

emps['year']  = emps['year'].astype(str)
emps['month'] = emps['month'].astype(str)
```

```
# separate column for first name and for last name:
emps['fname'],emps['lname'] = emps['name'].str.
split("-",1).str

# concatenate year and month with a "#" symbol:
emps['hdate1'] = emps['year'].
astype(str)+"#"+emps['month'].astype(str)

# concatenate year and month with a "-" symbol:
emps['hdate2'] = emps[['year','month']].agg('-'.join,
axis=1)

print(emps)
print()
```

Listing B.21 initializes the data frame df with the contents of the CSV file employees.csv, and then displays the contents of df. The next pair of code snippets invoke the astype() method to convert the contents of the year and month columns to strings.

The next code snippet in Listing B.21 uses the split() method to split the name column into the columns fname and lname that contain the first name and last name, respectively, of each employee's name:

```
emps['fname'],emps['lname'] = emps['name'].str.
split("-",1).str
```

The next code snippet concatenates the contents of the year and month string with a "#" character to create a new column called hdate1:

```
emps['hdate1'] = emps['year'].
astype(str)+"#"+emps['month'].astype(str)
```

The final code snippet concatenates the contents of the year and month string with a "-" to create a new column called hdate2, as shown here:

```
emps['hdate2'] = emps[['year','month']].agg('-'.join,
axis=1)
```

Now launch the code in Listing B.21 to see the following output:

emps:

```
        name     year month
0  Jane-Smith  2015.0   Aug
1  Dave-Smith  2020.0   Jan
2  Jane-Jones  2018.0   Dec
3  Jane-Stone  2017.0   Feb
4  Dave-Stone  2014.0   Apr
5  Mark-Aster     NaN   Oct
6  Jane-Jones     NaN   Jun
```

```
        name     year month fname  lname     hdate1
        hdate2
0  Jane-Smith  2015.0   Aug  Jane  Smith  2015.0#Aug
   2015.0-Aug
1  Dave-Smith  2020.0   Jan  Dave  Smith  2020.0#Jan
   2020.0-Jan
2  Jane-Jones  2018.0   Dec  Jane  Jones  2018.0#Dec
   2018.0-Dec
3  Jane-Stone  2017.0   Feb  Jane  Stone  2017.0#Feb
   2017.0-Feb
4  Dave-Stone  2014.0   Apr  Dave  Stone  2014.0#Apr
   2014.0-Apr
5  Mark-Aster     nan   Oct  Mark  Aster     nan#Oct
   nan-Oct
6  Jane-Jones     nan   Jun  Jane  Jones     nan#Jun
   nan-Jun
```

There is one other detail regarding the following commented out code snippet:

```
#emps['fname'],emps['lname'] = emps['name'].str.
split("-",1).str
```

The following deprecation message is displayed if you uncomment the preceding code snippet:

```
#FutureWarning: Columnar iteration over characters
#will be deprecated in future releases.
```

READING HTML WEB PAGES IN PANDAS

Listing B.22 displays the contents of the HTML Web page `abc.html`, and Listing B.23 shows the contents of `read_html_page.py` that illustrates how to read the contents of an HTML Web page from `Pandas`. Note that this code will only work with Web pages that contain *at least* one HTML `<table>` element.

Listing B.22: abc.html

```
<html>
<head>
</head>
<body>
  <table>
    <tr>
      <td>hello from abc.html!</td>
    </tr>
  </table>
</body>
</html>
```

Listing B.23: read_html_page.py

```
import pandas as pd

file_name="abc.html"
with open(file_name, "r") as f:
  dfs = pd.read_html(f.read())

print("Contents of HTML Table(s) in the HTML Web
Page:")
print(dfs)
```

Listing B.23 starts with an `import` statement, followed by initializing the variable `file_name` to `abc.html` that is displayed in Listing B.22. The next code snippet initializes the variable `dfs` as a data frame with the contents of the HTML Web page `abc.html`. The final portion of Listing B.19 displays the contents of the data frame `dsf`. Now launch the code in Listing B.23 to see the following output:

Contents of HTML Table(s) in the HTML Web Page:
[0
0 hello from abc.html!]

For more information about the `Pandas read_html()` method, navigate to this URL:

https://pandas.pydata.org/pandas-docs/stable/reference/api/

SAVING A PANDAS DATAFRAME AS AN HTML WEB PAGE

Listing B.24 shows the contents of `read_html_page.py` that illustrates how to read the contents of an HTML Web page from `Pandas`. Note that this code will only work with Web pages that contain at least one HTML `<table>` element.

Listing B.24: read_html_page.py

```
import pandas as pd

emps = pd.read_csv("employees.csv")
print("emps:")
print(emps)
print()

emps['year']  = emps['year'].astype(str)
emps['month'] = emps['month'].astype(str)

# separate column for first name and for last name:
emps['fname'],emps['lname'] = emps['name'].str.
split("-",1).str

# concatenate year and month with a "#" symbol:
emps['hdate1'] = emps['year'].
astype(str)+"#"+emps['month'].astype(str)

# concatenate year and month with a "-" symbol:
emps['hdate2'] = emps[['year','month']].agg('-'.join,
axis=1)
```

```
print(emps)
print()

html = emps.to_html()
print("Data frame as an HTML Web Page:")
print(html)
```

Listing B.24 populates the data frame `temps` with the contents of `employees.csv`, and then converts the `year` and `month` attributes to type string. The next code snippet splits the contents of the `name` field with the "-" symbol as a delimiter. As a result, this code snippet populates the new "fname" and "lname" fields with the first name and last name, respectively, of the previously split field.

The next code snippet in Listing B.24 converts the `year` and `month` fields to strings, and then concatenates them with a "#" as a delimiter. Yet another code snippet populates the `hdate2` field with the concatenation of the year and month fields.

After displaying the content of the data frame `emps`, the final code snippet populate the variable `html` with the result of converting the data frame `emps` to an HTML web page by invoking the `to_html()` method of `Pandas`. Now launch the code in Listing B.24 to see the following output:

```
Contents of HTML Table(s)
emps:
          name      year month
0   Jane-Smith    2015.0   Aug
1   Dave-Smith    2020.0   Jan
2   Jane-Jones    2018.0   Dec
3   Jane-Stone    2017.0   Feb
4   Dave-Stone    2014.0   Apr
5   Mark-Aster       NaN   Oct
6   Jane-Jones       NaN   Jun
```

	name	year	month	fname	lname	hdate1	hdate2
0	Jane-Smith	2015.0	Aug	Jane	Smith	2015.0#Aug	2015.0-Aug
1	Dave-Smith	2020.0	Jan	Dave	Smith	2020.0#Jan	2020.0-Jan

2	Jane-Jones 2018.0-Dec	2018.0	Dec	Jane	Jones	2018.0#Dec	
3	Jane-Stone 2017.0-Feb	2017.0	Feb	Jane	Stone	2017.0#Feb	
4	Dave-Stone 2014.0-Apr	2014.0	Apr	Dave	Stone	2014.0#Apr	
5	Mark-Aster nan-Oct	nan	Oct	Mark	Aster	nan#Oct	
6	Jane-Jones nan-Jun	nan	Jun	Jane	Jones	nan#Jun	

Data frame as an HTML Web Page:

```html
<table border="1" class="data frame">
  <thead>
    <tr style="text-align: right;">
      <th></th>
      <th>name</th>
      <th>year</th>
      <th>month</th>
      <th>fname</th>
      <th>lname</th>
      <th>hdate1</th>
      <th>hdate2</th>
    </tr>
  </thead>
  <tbody>
    <tr>
      <th>0</th>
      <td>Jane-Smith</td>
      <td>2015.0</td>
      <td>Aug</td>
      <td>Jane</td>
      <td>Smith</td>
      <td>2015.0#Aug</td>
      <td>2015.0-Aug</td>
    </tr>
```

```
    <tr>
      <th>1</th>
      <td>Dave-Smith</td>
      <td>2020.0</td>
      <td>Jan</td>
      <td>Dave</td>
      <td>Smith</td>
      <td>2020.0#Jan</td>
      <td>2020.0-Jan</td>
    </tr>
    // details omitted for brevity
    <tr>
      <th>6</th>
      <td>Jane-Jones</td>
      <td>nan</td>
      <td>Jun</td>
      <td>Jane</td>
      <td>Jones</td>
      <td>nan#Jun</td>
      <td>nan-Jun</td>
    </tr>
  </tbody>
</table>
```

SUMMARY

This appendix introduced you to `Pandas` for creating labeled data frames and displaying metadata of data frames. Then you learned how to create data frames from various sources of data, such as random numbers and hard-coded data values. In addition, you saw how to perform column-based and row-based operations in `Pandas` DataFrames.

You also learned how to read `Excel` spreadsheets and perform numeric calculations on the data in those spreadsheets, such as the minimum, mean, and maximum values in numeric columns. Then, you saw how to create `Pandas` DataFrames from data stored in `CSV` files.

INDEX

www.ingramcontent.com/pod-product-compliance
Lightning Source LLC
LaVergne TN
LVHW062310060326
832902LV00013B/2139